Let's Go Adventuring

25 EXCITING TRIPS AROUND INDIA

Supriya Sehgal is a Mumbai-based travel writer who has written for several international and Indian publications. She is also the author of *A Tigress Called Machhli and Other True Animal Stories from India*. Her favourite experiences include enjoying a big bowl of crunchy ant chutney in Chhattisgarh, swimming with sharks in Sri Lanka, spotting shy anteaters and flying in a four-seater plane with an open window on a rainy day in Guyana.

SUPRIYA SEHGAL

Let's Go Adventuring

25 Exciting Trips Around India

Illustrations by Sharanya Kunnath

hachette INDIA

First published in 2019 by Hachette India
(Registered name: Hachette Book Publishing India Pvt. Ltd)
An Hachette UK company
www.hachetteindia.com

SRD

ISBN 978-93-88322-72-0

Hachette Book Publishing India Pvt. Ltd
4th & 5th Floors, Corporate Centre
Plot No. 94, Sector 44, Gurugram – 122003, India

Typeset in Bembo Std 12/14.8
by Manmohan Kumar, Delhi

Printed and bound in India
by Manipal Tchnologies Limited, Manipal

FSC www.fsc.org
MIX
Paper from responsible sources
FSC™ C043100

Contents

Introduction

When the travel bug bites you, you can't wait to pack your bags and head out at any given opportunity. Even when you're coming back from a trip, you're already planning the next one. Travel does take over your mind if you love meeting interesting people, seeing ancient monuments or visiting odd temples, history-rich mosques, gurdwaras or even cemeteries. Personally, I'm partial to hikes, rafting, treks and anything that involves the ocean (even though I can't swim)!

The travel bug bite bit me in 2004. It was a weekend in Bengaluru, and I was done seeing all the places in the city – the temples, the lakes, the gardens, the museums… everything. I wondered to myself: *What next? What new places can I see now?* That evening, I went to the bus stop with no plan or destination in mind and played a version of Pin the Tail on the Donkey by shutting my eyes and moving my finger over a list of places that the overnight buses went to. When I stopped, my finger was pointing to a place called Mahe. This very small town (all of nine square kilometres) is surrounded by Kerala on three sides and the Arabian Sea on its fourth side. I hopped onto a bus that was going to Mahe, got there very early in the morning and spent two days walking around the town. I decided that for a change, I would discover things only by talking to people, so the Google tab on my phone remained firmly shut!

I met some fantastic folks whom I became friends with on the spot and who took me around (we still stay in touch). We went to a fishing village, an art school, an island close by and a flat-as-a-book beach, which one could even drive on, and an ancient temple surrounded by jackfruit trees. I was even invited to lunch at someone's house and to tea with 90-year-old lady who'd wanted to join the circus when she was young! In the olden days, many people from this region had been circus performers. The Mahe oldies told me that this town was once under the French administration, so a lot of people still spoke French here. They even tried teaching me some, but I'm quite bad at learning new languages, so I got stuck at bonjour (it means 'Good Morning') and a couple of other words. Mahe was the first odd but delightful town that featured first on my travels. There was no stopping after that.

Since then I've had the chance to travel to remote forests in India, climb mountains, go sailing in the sea and glide through clouds. But the best part really is the fact that I get to meet so many interesting people.

I hope you enjoy these 25 travel tales from my favourite experiences in India – which range from walking jelly-kneed on high rickety bridges and discovering cool temples and crazy monuments to trying something adventurous on my plate – like a full serving of red ants with their eggs! And these are all things you can do too with the help of a trained guide and places you get to easily enough with your travel companions.

Unfortunately, Mahe doesn't feature in this book, but I do hope you can go there some day. There are so many ridiculously exciting places to see in the country. Hopefully this book will inspire you to start exploring and adventuring right away.

I leave you with a *s'amuser*, which is 'have fun' in French. It's the other word I learnt in Mahe!

Fantastic Festivals

A Battle on the Backwaters

I've spent the last 15 years of my life travelling around India and the world, and it's really, *really* hard for me to pick a favourite destination. I've been lucky enough to see beautiful places with towering mountains piercing the sky; clear, blue oceans with thousands of fish and fascinating marine creatures; and dense jungles where the sunlight can't really reach the ground through the thick canopies of the trees and the only things you can hear are growls, squeaks and chirps. I've also had the chance to see colourful festivals, graceful dance performances, 24-hour prayer recitals, kite-flying competitions and more. So, whenever someone asks me which part of India is my favourite, I am *always* confused and take very long to answer!

But just a little while ago, during a trip, I found my answer – I found my favourite place! Now there'll be no more scratching my head in public and seeming a little silly.

Wondering what it is? Why don't you take a guess? Come on, I'll give you five clues. (And no peeking ahead!)

1. It's a town located in a state whose name starts with the letter K!
2. The name of the town starts with the letter A!
3. There are coconut trees everywhere in this town – and the state too!
4. There is a network of canals running through it!
5. It's where a most exciting battle on water takes place every year!

★

★

★

★

★

★

★

★

★

★

I'm talking about Alappuzha, or Alleppey! A small town located in the belly of Kerala, it lies along the Arabian Sea and is famous for the hundreds of narrow canals that run through it, crossing each other at every turn. (Think of them as watery roads.)

The backwaters of Kerala are a geographical wonder, and are made up of a massive network of salty lagoons, lakes, canals and rivers that lie parallel to the Arabian Sea. The backwaters are unique as they are formed by the action of waves and sea currents that create shallow islands at the mouths of rivers flowing into this sea. This leads to the formation of thin canals around these islands. These canals are interconnected, and form more than 900 kilometres of waterways in Kerala! When you explore them by boat, it doesn't seem like they're that long, but that's because the canals do not lie in a straight line – they curve and swing around like snakes. The waterways are flanked by waving coconut trees laden with green fruits clustered on top of large leaves that radiate out like the sun.

The areas surrounding the backwaters are filled with tropical plants and paddy fields. On both sides of the canals, there are local homes, churches, temples, shops and schools, so you can always see some activity – people bathing in the water, washing utensils and clothes, children going to school, and fishermen sitting patiently on the edges with their fishing rods, waiting to catch fresh fish for dinner. Some fishermen throw their nets into the water from a boat, spreading them out wide to their full size. I love the sight of these nets falling into the water with a splash!

My favourite thing about the backwaters is the hundreds of bridges constructed for people to walk from one bank to another. If you're going under a bridge in a boat, you'd actually be close enough to wave at the people on the bridge. I must have done this a thousand times when I last visited!

As I'm sure you can imagine, life around the backwaters is usually very serene and peaceful – except when there is a huge battle planned in the canals. No, no, I don't mean a battle fought with guns or swords! This one is fought with oars. I'm talking about the snake boat races held in this region. Snakes, boats, battles, races – you must be confused. Let me explain.

A long, long time ago, these canals were not navigated by motorboats but by long, narrow wooden boats crafted from *aanjili thadi*, a local forest wood tree. In those days, the kings and their armies used these boats to get around the maze of backwater canals, especially when they had to fight enemies. These boats had better access inside the canals than any other mode of transportation. Some people say that King Devanarayana of Chembakassery introduced these boats. Today, the tradition of gliding over the water on long, narrow boats is followed during the snake boat races that start in July and go on for the next six months. There are around 15 races in and around Alleppey each year, and I was lucky to see the most famous one – the Nehru Trophy Snake Boat Race.

Earlier, only a few races were held, but when the local villages saw the massive entertainment it was providing the community, they decided to launch their own races.

In the current racing scene, scores of villages send teams of more than 120 men on a single boat, with a singing troupe of six or eight men who sit in the middle. The singers encourage the men as they row. The captain stands in the middle or at the mast of the boat, which rises up like a snakehead (that's why the name 'snake boat'). He stands there at a height so he can have a full view of the boat and the track, and can steer the boat in the right direction and keep telling the oarsmen what to do. The teams are made up of regular villagers (carpenters, farmers, vegetable sellers, shop owners... basically, anyone who can row a boat). They practise for weeks before the main event, and on the day of the race, they come to the main venue (a canal) along with other boatloads of their fellow village folk who cheer them on.

The Nehru Trophy Snake Boat Race is held on the second Saturday of August every year. Thousands of people come to Alleppey on this day and stand along the Punnamada stretch, where the canal doesn't twist and turn but runs in a straight line. The racetrack on the water canal is about a kilometre long. Since many teams participate, the races go on from 10 a.m. till about 2 p.m. Four boats race each other at a time.

The boats make a grand entry! Each one has more than 120 men, and their energy is infectious (in a good way!). All the oars come splashing down into the water in time with each other, and the rhythm matches the song of the troupe on the boat. The song goes something like this: '*Dhit dhit tara, dhit dhit thai*' – pause – '*thai dhai, thag dhit dhit tom*'. The battle for the winner's position is intense as the winning team gets a cash award, and it is a matter of great pride for the oarsmen to represent their village.

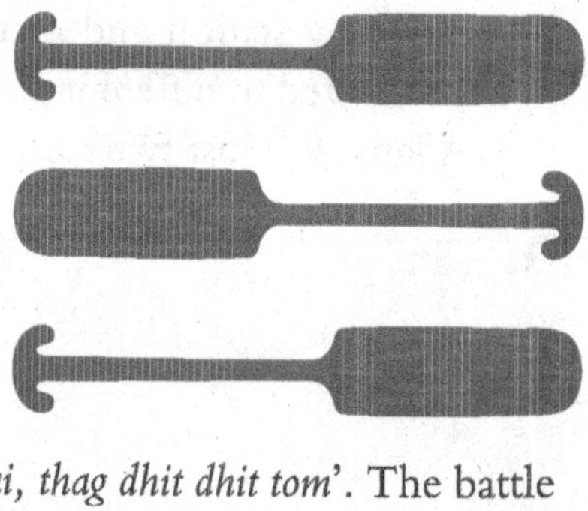

I think it's more fun to be on the edges and watch the boats zoom by. While the teams work hard on the

Alleppey backwaters, being in the stands is very different. The audience comes prepared with snacks and drinks for the day, and everyone, from old people to little children, sits on the sides of the canal. The very green backwaters are suddenly painted in hundreds of colours, and loud cheers fill the air. Playful banter with other villagers, teasing and jokes are part of the celebrations of the day – it's like a big party where everyone seems to know each other! And that's why this is one of my favourite places. After all, who doesn't like a big party?

How to Get to Alleppey

You will first have to get to Ernakulam (also known as Kochi). Ernakulam has an airport, a railway station and many bus stands that are connected to different parts of India. And then, Alleppey is just two hours away.

A Legend about Snake Boats

There is an interesting legend around the snake boat races in Kerala. It is said that a long time ago, a Brahmin was waiting to complete his daily ritual of giving food to a poor person, but no poor person came that day. The Brahmin was very worried, so he started praying to Lord Krishna. After a while, a young boy appeared, asking for food. The Brahmin happily fed him, but the moment he finished, the boy disappeared and was later seen at the Aranmula Temple (about 52 kilometres from Alleppey). The Brahmin realized that the boy had been Lord Krishna himself! From then on, people started bringing food to offer in this temple in long boats. The Aranmula Temple is one of the oldest temples in the region, and the snake boat race of Aranmula is also very famous.

The Hornbill Festival

Five minutes after the dance had begun, my first thought was that it looked a bit awkward. A man wearing only a short red skirt and a feathery headdress hopped about the stage in strange skips, shouting words that made little sense: 'Phoo, phoo, phoo, aa, aa, aa!' And the audience just kept clapping and cheering him on! I was really confused about what they were enjoying about the performance. The dance was not graceful. And the dancer was not matching his steps to any beat or music. Was I missing something? I tapped a young boy standing near me on the shoulder and asked him what was going on. He explained that the man on stage had just eaten 30 *bhut jolokia* chillies in one minute and was now jumping around because his mouth was burning!

Bhut jolokia, also known as the ghost pepper, is one of the world's hottest chilli peppers, capable of scorching your mouth if you ate it and singeing your hands if you touched it without gloves! *Why on earth would someone eat 30 of these chillies?* And why was *I* at such a competition?

Well, I had just entered the annual Hornbill Festival in Kohima, Nagaland, in the hope of seeing some traditional dances and music performances, but I had landed up at the chilli-eating competition instead! One after the other, men came up on stage, grabbed a bunch of chillies and did the jump-hop-aaa dance around the platform. (But no one seemed to be able to beat that score of 30 yet!)

Nagaland is on the north-eastern edge of India. Did you know that Assam, Meghalaya, Arunachal Pradesh, Tripura, Mizoram, Nagaland and Manipur are together called the Seven Sisters? Now Sikkim is also part of the gang, but people still call it Seven Sisters! The communities in each state share some similarities but are otherwise quite different in terms of culture and traditions. Nagaland has 16 different tribal groups – all of whom have unique eating habits, special languages and even completely different clothing. The Hornbill Festival in Nagaland is celebrated during the first ten days of December every year. The festival is named after the Great Indian Hornbill, a large and colourful bird that features in the folklore of the state's tribes. All 16 tribes come to the capital, Kohima, from different regions, and have one big party, in which they perform traditional dances, sing songs, cook their

special dishes and put up stalls of their handicrafts, like shawls, stoles and utensils. They also have competitions like the chilli-eating one and wrestling. On the last day, all the tribes come together to dance around a bonfire in the closing ceremony.

The Naga Tribes

The names of the tribes are Angami, Ao, Chakhesang, Chang, Kachari, Khiamniungan, Konyak, Kuki, Lotha, Phom, Pochury, Rengma, Sangtam, Sumi, Yimchunger and Zeme-Liangmai. These tribes once lived in remote areas of the Nagaland Hills. They were essentially hunter-gatherers, which means they lived off forests and farmlands.

The festival is a great place to see the unique dances, songs, food and lifestyles of the different Naga tribes. The Naga people wear extremely colourful clothes, and the headgear is the most interesting part of their traditional costume. Some tribes wear a crown made of arrows that stand up straight; others make the headdress more beautiful by decorating it with bird feathers, beads and other items. They also wear fascinating jewellery, like necklaces with metal beads, feathers, bones and skull-shaped ornaments.

I had planned to be in Kohima for the last two days of the Hornbill Festival. On the first day, I strolled around the venue at about 11 a.m. and looked at the *morungs* assigned to each tribe. A *morung* is a traditional wooden cottage found in the villages of Nagaland, which doubled up as a hostel in the olden days. Here, young boys (mostly teenagers) would spend a few years learning how to hunt, sing and dance and also the traditional ways of living from the older boys. Since there was no school in those days, this was the way young children learnt from the elders. While the boys stayed in hostels, the girls learnt from their mothers and older sisters at home. This doesn't happen anymore, but each village still has *morungs*. The festival organizers had constructed 16 *morungs* for visitors to get a glimpse of how the Nagas once lived.

I went into the Angami *morung*, where a large kitchen with a central fireplace took up most of the space. Angamis are one of the major tribes of Nagaland; they live around Kohima and Dimapur. Everyone from the tribe had gathered there and were relaxing until it was their turn to perform. They were cooking local dishes, and yummy smells wafted through the air, tempting me. I bought myself a plate of *aikibeye* (a mustard-leaf dish), boiled rice and pork curry, and settled down around the fire to chat with the people of the Angami tribe. The food was so delicious that I had to get myself a second helping!

The second part of my day (after lunch) was spent roaming around the handicraft stalls and seeing some spirited dances (real, proper dances, not like the chilli-eating ones!), where men and women moved to an easy beat, moving their bodies lightly and dancing in mostly a circle. By 5 p.m., the sky turned inky (the sun sets very early in Nagaland) and the day came to a close.

On the last day of the festival, everyone cheered and wished each other luck until they met again next December. Remember the closing ceremony I mentioned a little while ago? Well, in the afternoon, around 20 people from the 16 tribes gathered around a huge bonfire and danced together one last time. It must have taken a lot of practice as they all matched steps and stayed to the beats. They also called all the visitors to join them in the last dance. The headman of the Angami tribe, whom I had met earlier, asked me to join too!

I could certainly dance a little, but if he'd asked me to be part of the *bhut-jolokia*-eating contest, I'd have run in the opposite direction!

How to Reach the Hornbill Festival

You can fly into Dimapur Airport, which is about 75 kilometres from Kohima. Make sure you and your travel companions book a room at one of the hotels as early as possible because thousands of people come to see this festival every year.

Other Things to See in Kohima

- **Kohima War Cemetery:** This is a well-kept cemetery where Allied soldiers who died in World War II are buried.
- **Nagaland State Museum:** Visit the state museum of Nagaland to see a treasure trove of Naga artefacts.
- **Khonoma:** This village is about 20 kilometres from Kohima and is known for its beauty, love for nature and strict rules for keeping everything green. No hunting of wild animals and birds or cutting of trees is allowed in this village. And there is a dustbin at every corner of the streets. What a great example to set in terms of nature conservation!

The Gods Who Bunk School

When I was in school in Dehradun, we used to get two full months of summer holidays and one month for winter. It was 90 days of sheer bliss! I would get up really late and roam around in my jammies for hours after breakfast. I played with my dog, fed the two cows in the shed behind the house, called friends over for a game of cricket or hide-and-seek, and wandered about in the orchard next to my home until my mother yelled at me to come back and bathe. And sometimes, I even forgot to bathe the *whole* day. But I was still greedy for more ultra-lazy days, and I'd keep praying and praying for unexpected holidays in the middle of the year.

So can you imagine my jealousy when I met someone who loves holidays as much as me and gets an entire month off from school right in the middle of the term? Who is this lucky soul?

I'm talking about an extremely special kid called Ganesh, and he lives in a town called Ramnagar.

Next to the more famous religious city of Varanasi, known for ancient temples and the River Ganga flowing through it, there is a small town called Ramnagar. Large numbers of travellers visit Varanasi every year to see these temples and bathe in the Ganga (it's considered a holy river, and people believe that by bathing in it, they will be able to wash away their sins). And poor old Ramnagar doesn't feature in many itineraries – it's a sleepy place with dusty, dirty roads and an old, crumbling fort called the Ramnagar Fort at the edge of the same river that winds round Varanasi. It's only in October every year that this otherwise quiet town sees a lot of excitement. The month leading up to Dussehra is bursting with activity.

Every year, a group of actors enact the main episodes of the Ramayana for the people of Ramnagar, as part of an old tradition. This performance is known as Ramlila. Many other towns like Delhi, Ayodhya, Vrindavan, Almora and Madhubani also follow this tradition, but it's quite special in Ramnagar. Here, each day before Dussehra is assigned to one major episode of the story. And all the actors are children. The people in the town make different stages and backdrops for Ayodhya, Janakpur and Lanka, the cities that feature in the story – like an orchard, a lakeside field, a proper stage, a temple and many other types of locations. The actors learn up their dialogues pretty well, but a part of the story is told by bhajan singers (adults in this case) as the plot progresses.

Wait, wait, there's more! When the actors need to be moved from location to location for different scenes, they are carried on the shoulders of these singers. The entire audience, made up of thousands of people, follows them around. The performers stop and perform, and then move to the next part. Wait, I'm still not done! There is another incredible thing about this performance of the Ramlila. None of the actors or singers use any microphones. All the dialogues are spoken loudly, and all the songs are sung with great gusto. Naturally, the audience at the back can barely hear but that's okay. Tradition is tradition. The audience also includes the king of Ramnagar, and he follows this troupe of actors and singers on an elephant. Can you imagine this whole spectacle? Well, I think it's simply amazing!

About five years ago, I travelled to the town to see this unique Ramlila. I arrived a few days before the performance was supposed to start, and decided to go look at the different stages that were being created. Wooden planks were being carried around, carpenters were hard at work, flower decorations were underway, and Ramnagar didn't look sleepy at all. Tired after a whole morning of walking in the blazing heat, I decided to rest in an old temple by the river. It didn't look like a very popular place as there were no queues, no stalls and not even a temple bell hanging outside. In fact, the main door seemed shut, but there was a shaded veranda built all around the temple, and it looked really inviting in the heat of the day.

Walking in, I plonked myself on the cool ground and was taking a sip of water, when the main door creaked open and someone peered out at me. A red-faced kid ran out and then swiftly hid again. He was back in a couple of seconds and then he disappeared *again*. I followed him to say hi and opened the heavy door of the temple. Inside, the main sprawling courtyard was buzzing with action. Lots of young children between the ages of nine and 13 were dressed as the cast of the Ramayana.

I spotted the red-faced kid, and he gave me a big toothy smile. That's when I noticed the long tail stuck behind him. *He must be Hanuman*, I thought. The main characters – Ram, Sita and a blue-bodied Lakshman – were huddled in a corner, practising their dialogues together. While I was looking at this busy scene, someone tapped my shoulder. It was a priest wearing a white dhoti and a crisp, clean kurta. He had a small ponytail that bobbed up and down as he spoke to me. When he found out why I was visiting the place, he offered to chat with me for a while.

The priest explained that I had entered the dress rehearsal of the Ramlila for the year. There were only a few days to go until the final performance, and everyone was quite busy with the preparations. He introduced me to some of the characters, 'This is Ganesh, our Ram for this year.' The Sita character had fallen sick the last minute, so the new Sita had to work extra hard to learn the dialogues. She looked pretty stressed and had no time to smile or wave hello. There were many kids dressed like

the Hanuman character because the story has a whole army of monkeys!

The priest told me that the people of Ramnagar considered these children holy for this month and even worshipped them. No one was allowed to touch them or talk to them too much. After all, they were going to be gods and goddesses! They had to skip school (the lucky, lucky children!) and stay a whole month in this temple under his care. They revised their dialogues every day, practised the scenes and played gods the whole time.

It was time for the rehearsal now, so I had to leave, but before going, I snuck in a quick conversation with the child playing Ram.

'Psssst!' I called out to him. 'What's your name? Do you like playing Ram?'

He nodded excitedly and smiled.

'But you live away from your home for a whole month! Don't you miss it?'

'That's okay,' said Ganesh aka Ram. 'It also means I don't have to go to school.' And his grin widened. Ganesh was clearly just like me.

How to Get to Ramnagar

The best way to get to Ramnagar is by first getting to Varanasi and then using a boat or a cab to travel the last stretch. Varanasi is connected by flights, trains and buses to many major and small cities of India. The boat ride to Ramnagar from Varanasi takes about 45 minutes.

Things to See in and around Ramnagar

- **Ramnagar Fort & Museum:** This is the town's main fort and museum.
- **Sarnath:** This famous town nearby is known for its Buddhist stupas.
- **Sunrise in Varanasi:** A boat ride during sunrise is a lovely experience. There is a lot of activity amidst the hundreds of small and big temples on the edge of the Ganga River.

Eating Ant Chutney

Jogna, the headman of the village of Tokapal, pushed a bowl made of leaves towards me. I peered into the leafy cup holding a mysterious red-and-white paste. That's when I saw that the ingredients had heads and legs mish-mashed together. When I shot Jogna a questioning glance, he smiled and said, 'Eat, eat. It's delicious!'

I was still a little suspicious, so I asked him what it was. With a huge grin, he told me that it was a chutney made of red ants and their white eggs! *What?* And these weren't even the tiny ones. These were the big ants that bite really hard. So what if they'd been squished in a mortar and pestle...what if one was alive and bit my tongue? This was straight out of a nightmare – my food biting me instead of the other way round!

But Jogna assured me that all of them were most certainly dead, and that this chutney was the yummiest thing I would eat in Bastar. I took the plunge and grabbed a spoon (also made of leaves) and took a big bite.

Tangy, crunchy, tickly, salty – a number of words came to mind, but I could not deny that the chutney was indeed quite yummy!

I was in Jagdalpur in the Bastar district for a festival called Bastar Dussehra. Bastar is a region in southern Chhattisgarh, and Jagaldpur is the main town there. In fact, it is the *only* town. The rest of Bastar only has small villages occupied by tribal people – the Murias, Bison Horn Marias, the extremely shy Abhuj Marias, Bhatras, Dhurvas, Gadbas, Dorlas and Halbas. Many of them live deep in the jungles and live on fruits and food that they grow. They don't like to come to the town, except for weekly *haat*s (markets) and the Bastar Dussehra. This annual festival is celebrated for 75 days, when all the tribals travel from distant villages to Jagdalpur to pay homage to their main deity, Danteshwari. The grand festival is a treasure trove of legends and fascinating rituals spread across months.

I had been in Bastar for over 72 days, but I had not had the ant chutney until my guide, Awesh Ali, took me to Jogna's house in a village close to Jagdalpur. Nothing much was going to happen back at the festival grounds in the town until evening, so we'd decided that we would spend the day visiting other villages. We walked around homes made of mud, crossed a paddy field and saw some local shrines, where the gods were also mostly made of mud. Seeing unfamiliar faces in his village, Jogna had called out to us and invited us home for some snacks.

The ant chutney is a staple of the tribals of Chhattisgarh, as it helps them get rid of illnesses, especially fever and cold. They have a pretty cool way of collecting these ants. The red ants make their nests on the top of trees, and the tribals climb these and shake the nests till they fall. The ants don't fall on the ground, because another person stands below the tree with a cloth spread out in front of them and catches the nests. The ants fall everywhere like rain, so the collector has to be quick. The collector then wraps them in a leaf, folds it to keep them from running away and then squishes them in a mortar and pestle. Ginger, salt and red ants – the perfect way to eat *bhajjis*! Jogna told me that these ants have a particular chemical in them (known as formic acid), which helps to get rid of fever and a number of other illnesses.

After some more snacks and conversation with Jogna, Awesh and I thanked him and left for the festival ground. It was an important day in the festival calendar. As a run-up to the festival, a huge chariot is built with the contribution of different tribals. Some of them provide the wood, others the decorations, and some work as carpenters. On the third-last day, the massive chariot, which is as big as a *house*, is pulled around the town by hundreds of men, the idol of Goddess Danteshwari resting on it.

While most of the action happens in the evening, there is still an air of festivity in the day. The tribals put up a number of stalls on the side of the only main road in town. Handicrafts and food are the main things on display, and some tribals come to barter the vegetables and fruits they grow in the jungle for clothes and jewellery.

Since there was still time for the chariot-pulling to begin, Awesh and I decided to walk down the street looking at the different crafts – like bell metal curios, stone sculptures, terracotta toys and silver jewellery.

At one point, I noticed a small group of people huddled on the side of the road, everyone sitting on their haunches. When we got closer, I peeped through the gaps between the people and saw a lady using a nail and hammer to make a tattoo on another girl's forehead. Not arm, not leg, but forehead! It looked pretty painful to me, but the brave girl who was being tattooed had a peaceful expression on her face. In fact, she gave me a wide grin when the tattoo was complete.

Awesh told me that a lot of tribals in the state get themselves tattooed. I had seen many women with dots and other designs made on their arms and legs, but this was the first time I'd seen it on someone's forehead. Awesh also told me that only the Baigas from the north of Chhattisgarh and parts of Madhya Pradesh did this in order to identify the different stages of a woman's life. For example, when a woman gets married, she gets one symbol tattooed on her body; when she has a child, something else is added to the design.

When I asked Awesh if people ever got infections, he smiled and said, 'The ant chutney helps them with that as well – no infections, nothing!'

Getting to Jagdalpur

Raipur, the capital of Chhattisgarh, is connected by air, rail and road to major cities of India. From here, one can take a cab or a bus to go south to Jagdalpur. It takes about six hours to traverse the belly of the state over a beautiful drive filled with intense greenery.

Things to See in and around Jagdalpur

- **Chitrakote Waterfall:** This waterfall's seven streams come cascading down 95 feet. There are lots of other waterfalls in this region, but this is the most famous one.
- **Kanger Valley National Park:** Rugged mountains, thundering waterfalls, dense forests… there's no reason to not visit this place!
- **Irikpal:** Irikpal is about 22 kilometres from Jagdalpur and is known for a craft called cowrie shell work. When you go to this village, you will see women attaching bright white shells to their colourful skirts, blouses, bags and hats in order to decorate them.

The Goddess of Kodungallur

When I was young (well, younger than I am right now), my mother always glared at me the moment a bad word slipped out of my mouth. There were many words that I was absolutely not allowed to say, and the most that I could trouble my elder sister with was words like 'stupid' or 'donkey'! So I had a special name for her – Spiggy (a mash-up of the words 'stupid' and 'piggy'). The best part was that my mother didn't figure it out for a long time!

But even calling my sister Spiggy wasn't fun after some time, and I needed something more annoying. When I was nine years old, a certain *really bad* word almost came out of my mouth while arguing with her, which was immediately followed by a hard slap on the back of my head. My mom had been standing behind me all the time, her forehead knotted in irritation with our constant bickering. Aaargh! I was stopped right in the nick of time. Sometimes it's just nice to have a spat with your sibling and get it over with. I wish I'd known about the temple I'm going to tell you about then – I would have been able to tell my mother that it was okay to say bad words sometimes. Because, believe it or not, devotees at this temple in Kerala get a whole day to call the chief goddess all kinds of names!

When I heard about this unique tradition, I planned a trip to the town of Kodungallur in Kerala at once to visit the temple. Kodungallur is a small, sleepy town on the edge of the Arabian Sea with one very important address – the Sri Kurumba Bhagavathy Temple. The temple complex is massive, with a dry muddy area in front. At the end of it stands a massive banyan tree, and next to this is a large house-like structure with sanctums of different gods and goddesses inside. The main deity here is the goddess Shakti, also known as Bhadrakali. The idol is made from the wood of the jackfruit tree and is about six feet tall and has eight arms. Important Hindu gods like Shiva, Ganapati and Veerabhadra also make an appearance in the other shrines, but Bhadrakali is the centre of attention here. (As I'm sure you already know, Indian gods and goddesses can have scores of versions. This goddess is also known as Kannaki or Kali.)

Now, I had planned to make this trip in April, so I could visit the temple during the Kodungallur Bharani Festival. When I reached the temple early in the morning on the day of the festival, all was calm. It didn't look like a place that would be bursting with energy and people anytime soon. A young priest named Hari, hanging around in the courtyard, saw me wandering about and came to offer me some information. 'Don't worry,' he said, looking at my puzzled expression, 'it will all start around 11 a.m.'

Luckily he didn't have too many priestly duties that day (only the senior priests did), so he had the time to explain the meaning of the various traditions at this temple to me. Hari told me that the festival is celebrated each year around March or April to honour the victory of the goddess Bhadrakali over a demon called Daarika. The temple was famous enough to have devotees all year round, but on this day, thousands of people would gather here – some from nearby villages, some from different states and some who were just curious travellers like me. After a while, Hari looked at his watch and said, 'I should expect the crowds to pour in any time.' He was right.

By 11.15 a.m., the temple complex had begun to fill up with people rapidly. But the most noticeable of them were the men and women dressed in red robes. They were holding sharp swords, their hair flying wildly, and a blob of yellow turmeric was smeared on their heads. Some of them wore a belt around their waists with bells hanging from it. Hari told me that they were oracles, people who could go into a trance, and it was believed that gods and goddesses spoke through these oracles.

Soon, the first ritual, called Kozhikkallu Moodal, started with some special members of the temple making offerings to the goddess. They sacrificed a rooster for this. This ceremony symbolizes the fight between the goddess and her opponent Daarika. Then it was time for the royal family of the region to pray at the main shrine, while all the others waited outside. By this time, some of the oracles (also known as Vellichapads) were already in a trance.

Hari and I placed ourselves near the corner of a pillar where no one could knock us down. Some of the oracles were running about with their swords pointed to the sky and their hair billowing. When I looked closely, I noticed that many of them had made cuts on their foreheads and then put turmeric on top of the cuts, but there was still blood trickling down their faces. While this looked a bit scary, Hari assured me that it was just their love and passion for the goddess that made them get into this frenzied mode.

Then came the part that I had been waiting for. Many of the oracles, after running around the temple, stood outside the sanctum and shouted in loud, jeering tones at the idol. I couldn't understand much since they were shouting in Malayalam, but I could tell these were no soft, gentle words of love. Hari smiled and told me that these were extremely bad words, but this act of swearing at the goddess was a tradition.

Even though I'd spent a whole day there, I was still a bit confused. Why on earth would they swear at a goddess they loved so much? Hari then explained to me that it was a day to test Bhadrakali's love for her devotees. The oracles believe that she is such a giving and warm-hearted goddess that she would continue to love them despite the bad words.

That's when I realized that this was the perfect excuse to present before my mother – if only she believed that I was swearing at my sister because I loved her too much. Although, something tells me that the whack on my head would just have come down with more force!

How to Get to Kodungallur

The Kodungallur temple lies around 27 kilometres from the city of Ernakulam. You can easily take a taxi from there to the temple. Make sure you get there around 8 a.m., before the crowds come in.

Temple Lore

The people of Kodungallur believe that this ancient shrine was once dedicated to Shiva, but the sage Parasuraman, who was once passing through this area, is said to have installed an idol of Bhadrakali alongside Shiva's. This is why the main idol at the complex is actually of Mahadev (Shiva), but Bhadrakali got so popular over the years with the devotees that now the temple has started being known as the Kodungallur Bhagavathy (another name for Bhadrakali) Temple.

Perfect Playgrounds

Zipping Down Snowy Slopes

Let the title of this chapter not confuse you. When I say 'zipping', I actually mean 'moving ahead at a snail's speed three or four feet and then falling down with an ungraceful THUD'. Basically, I landed on my bum, legs up in the air and elbows in the snow. Not the greatest-looking adventure sport photo, I know, but that was me last October, trying to learn skiing.

I had travelled to Srinagar from Delhi to write about the famous Dal Lake and its floating post office (I'll tell you about that later!). I had some extra time, so I decided to visit the nearby town of Gulmarg as well. Only an hour away from Srinagar, Gulmarg is a hill station that is part of the Western Himalayas. The town is at 8,690 feet from sea level, so it can get extremely cold. I was really looking forward to riding the cable car that connects the Kongdoori Peak (10,100 feet) and the Apharwat Peak

(13,800 feet) in Gulmarg. These two peaks are always topped with snow, no matter what time of the year it is. The slopes of these mountains are great for skiing, and many people from around the world come here to do exactly that. Who doesn't want to go zooming this way and that through the snowy slopes of a mountain? Sounds like a lot of fun, right? Well, you decide when you reach the end of this story.

Now I had NO plans of trying to whoosh down mountains while I was travelling to Gulmarg. But I do love trying out new things. When I reached the town, there was a fairly long queue for the cable car. While I was inching closer to the ticket counter, a pink-cheeked, sharp-nosed guide came to me and said (with the widest, warmest smile I had ever seen), 'Madam, you look like a true adventurer. Why don't you try skiing?'

Okay, I'll admit I was a bit flattered. So I smiled back and said, pointing to the pair of skis he was carrying on his shoulders, 'But I don't even know how to put them on!'

The guide, who introduced himself as Ashfaq, tried again. 'Don't you worry about that. I can teach you easily. You look like you're made for the mountains. Athletic, smart, light. It will be no problem teaching you!'

I beamed, but after another look at the skis, I weakly attempted to brush him away. Ashfaq wasn't one to give up so easily. He stayed with me till I reached the ticket counter, where I paid for his ticket as well, because he had convinced me by then that skiing was in my blood!

We sat in the cable car, and up we went with a slight jerk, till everything became smaller and smaller as we floated into the sky. The rickety cable car stopped at Kongdoori Peak so we could drop a few people off. Ashfaq and I had planned to continue to the highest point. He told me that he had been teaching people to ski for ten years and was such a good teacher that many travellers had become pros because of his expert lessons.

I found that I wasn't anxious at all. Even if I fell, I wasn't going to hurt myself, was I? The snow was so fluffy and soft! As we rose between the clouds, I forgot all about the skiing for a while. The town below us was tucked under a sheet of snow, and I have no words to describe the scene. I just stared and stared and stared. The people and the ponies who were ferrying them looked like little black dots, and the mountain peaks in the distance, each topped with a dollop of snow, looked like inverted V-shaped cakes with icing!

Finally, we arrived at the Apharwat Peak. Ashfaq let me take a few pictures and then asked me to step onto the skis so he could strap me in. Easy-peasy...so far.

The first time went like this: *Stand straight in the snow with the skis. Grip your ski poles. One leg front. The other leg to match it. And THUD!*

Ashfaq laughed and pulled me up. I laughed along. I was sure I'd get the hang of it soon.

Second time. *Left slide, pull yourself up with the poles, and bring the right leg ahead, then left. And THUD!* Even louder than the first time!

Okay, this wasn't going to be as simple as I thought.

Ashfaq decided it was time to show me how it was done by doing it himself. So he got onto his skis, went ahead for a few metres and then climbed back to where I stood. I'd followed his movement closely, so I took FIVE WHOLE STEPS on my town. Major progress – phew! Thankfully, I wasn't alone. In fact, I was surrounded by a whole lot of other disastrous learning attempts. But once in a while, an advanced person would swoosh down between all the learners, looking very cool, and all eyes would follow him or her, very jealously, down the slope.

After my tenth attempt, I asked Ashfaq to sit down and stop helping me get up every time. Poor thing, he must have got so bored talking encouragingly to me at every fall, when I knew I was quite terrible. He accepted the offer (with relief) and scurried off to get some tea for us from a nearby stall, while I continued with my routine of 'five steps and fall with a thud'.

I was now quite irritated. I was wet and sore, and had made no progress on the steps. But after a short tea break, I picked myself up with fresh energy and managed SEVEN steps before falling. Okay, some improvement. An hour had passed, and I was determined to do at least a small stretch.

Just when I was getting up for the thousandth time, someone suddenly came from behind and banged into me so hard that I slid 20 feet down one curve of the mountain. Unfortunately, my skis and poles were pointing to the sky, and the only connection to the mountain and the snow was my wet bum.

Ashfaq came skiing down and stopped where I had frantically managed to brake. 'I think you will need to practise for many days, Madam.' He looked at me sympathetically, though I could clearly see that he was trying to hide a laugh.

But I wasn't feeling bad at all. In fact, I was delighted! I had travelled 20 feet down the mountain slope in my skis. So what if my feet weren't actually touching the snow?

How to Get to Gulmarg

The closest airport to Gulmarg is located in Srinagar, which has many flights that connect it to different cities in India. You can land in Srinagar, hop into a taxi, and get to Gulmarg in an hour.

Dal Lake's Floating Post Office

Dal Lake is a sprawling lake in Srinagar and is often called 'Lake of Flowers' or 'Srinagar's Jewel'. It's a fascinating waterbody, as many people have built homes, shops and even a school on the small islands in the lake. People get around from one island to another in slim boats called *shikaras*. There is one floating object on this lake that gets a lot of attention from tourists. It's a floating post office! Manned by two or three employees, the post office glides around the lake, picking up and dropping off post. The post office also has a philately museum with a huge collection of unique stamps. And there's a souvenir shop too from where one can buy postcards, stamps and gifts for friends.

An Underwater Adventure

If you ask my friends to tell you something about me, the first thing they'll say is that I'm a beach bum! Addicted to the sun even if I'm burning up, I have a great love for sand, which is much stronger than my love for clouds. I have an equal amount of enthusiasm for marine life, especially octopuses and turtles. And yet, I've managed to spend most of my life without knowing how to swim. Even knee-deep water in a swimming pool makes me nervous, forget about the sea or a river!

And that's why my parents looked at me really *strangely* when I suggested we visit the Andaman and Nicobar Islands. 'You don't even know how to swim,' said my dad, frowning.

But I wanted to go for a few simple reasons. From what I'd heard about the place, there was clear, aquamarine water for as far as you could see and beautiful golden beaches straight out of my dreams.

I replied, 'Dad, imagine this if you can – a comfy lounger, shorts, fresh juice at hand and a newspaper. No hurry to get to work, nothing to worry about.'

The expression on his face immediately changed to a dreamy, hopeful one and before we knew it, we'd booked flight tickets from Delhi to Port Blair, the capital city of the Andaman and Nicobar islands.

The next stage, choosing where to stay, was a little confusing because there were literally hundreds of websites tempting us with images of cottages by the sea with unrestricted views of emerald waters. We finally zeroed in on a resort built at the edge of the blue ocean on Havelock Island. We were ready for the sun, sand and water!

The Andaman and Nicobar Islands are a cluster of 300 islands located in the Bay of Bengal. The small and big islands together make an idyllic picture – of palm-fringed beaches with white, soft sand, mangroves and tropical rainforests. The coral reefs in the sea are home to a diverse marine life, such as sharks, rays, trout, jobfish, turtles and hundreds of other creatures, making this an excellent place to go scuba diving and snorkelling.

We arrived in Port Blair, and were transported to Havelock Island by ferry. It was a two-hour ride over fairly choppy waters, most of which I spent regretting having eaten a big breakfast that morning. When we hopped out of the ferry onto the jetty, I could see the clear waters flowing under it. I even spotted a school of baby sharks swimming around calmly, as if they were familiar with the spot and tourists. Smiles spread on our faces, but it was only when we felt the soft talcum-powder-like sand under our feet and caught the view of the bright blue swimming pool in front of our rooms that the holiday really kicked in.

The bright blue-tiled pool, we learned, was the most coveted spot at the resort. Armed with towels, hats, sun glasses, books and sunscreen, we were the first to occupy the best beach beds on the side of the pool. But my dad kept making fun of me when my swimsuit was dry even after two hours. I finally got to the edge of the pool, and my mum and I dipped our legs in the warm water but didn't dare go in. We sipped our fresh juice and chatted merrily, while Dad read every word in the magazine that he had got from the reception.

Finally, the sun arched over us and settled into a spectacular sunset, dipping behind the horizon into the sea. That night, we debated if we should go snorkelling or diving, despite my fear of water. After all, we had not seen many fish on our first day, and a major part of the charm of the Andamans lay in the aquarium-like ambience of the islands. Now, even though I'm scared of water, I really did want to see the marine creatures that I had heard so much about. The only way to do that is to go snorkelling or diving with an instructor. The good part is that if you go diving, you don't have to know how to swim. There is an instructor who holds your hand at all times to help you balance underwater, and you have a big oxygen tank attached to you, so breathing underwater is easy. My mum encouraged me to give it a try and I booked a short snorkelling and diving trip for the next day. She even volunteered to come along and sit in the boat (as long as I didn't ask her to dangle her legs off it or anything).

Fortunately, the water around Havelock is largely without waves (it kind of feels like an oversized water tub with a base of soft white sand). But sadly, this was not where we would be diving. My mum and I joined the other tourists on a boat and travelled around 30 minutes to the location of the dive. My fear of the water was slowly going away after seeing how inviting the ocean looked. We were each assigned to an instructor and we were to dive only with them. After a short introduction to the hand gestures we would use to communicate underwater and how we should breathe using the equipment from the mouth, it was time to take the plunge! I said bye to my mum and jumped in with the instructor. This was a relatively isolated spot from the beaches, where the water was deep enough to jump in. There was a coral reef below, where we would be able to find many varieties of fish. A coral reef looks like a bunch of rocks, but actually reefs are tiny living organisms huddled together. A coral reef is like a large residential colony for some of the sea creatures.

At first, I was a little jittery about being immersed in the open ocean, but slowly my eyes adjusted to the beautiful canvas of marine life spread out in front of me. We found ourselves being

surrounded by schools of tiny fish – which never touched us – and seeing colours that we had never imagined. A group of Moorish idol fish passed us calmly, though the black-and-yellow butterfly fish seemed hesitant to get closer. Other fish, like the triggerfish, spotted dart and longnose hawkfish, continued to inspect the coral unaffected by our intrusion. I looked around plenty but there was no sign of a turtle or an octopus. An hour must have passed as we gazed at the traffic of marine creatures. And then, just when I was taking one last look around, I saw it – a full-bellied turtle in all its glory gliding past me!

Smiling broadly under my mask, I gestured to the instructor with an A-okay sign. He gave me a thumbs up and pointed at something else that I had missed. Another creature was scuttling past the base of some coral, throwing sand in every direction. It was a full-grown octopus! If the breathing pipes had been released from my mouth, I would have squealed with happiness. But that, of course, would have been a very silly thing to do!

How to Get to Andaman & Nicobar Islands

You can take a direct flight to Port Blair from most major cities in India. Once you get there, you can get into a private boat or hop aboard a large ferry to visit the different islands. Havelock Island is the most popular spot for tourists as it has many resorts, hotels and restaurants.

Pottering about Port Blair

- **Samudrika Naval Marine Museum:** This is a special museum with exhibits on the ocean environment.
- **Light and Sound Show at the Cellular Jail:** This jail is where Indian freedom fighters were once imprisoned, especially during the British Raj.
- **Birdwatching:** You can go to the Chidiya Tapu Beach for birdwatching. Make sure you go with a guide.
- **Aberdeen Bazaar:** This is a great place to wander about in the evening and pick up souvenirs for friends back home.

Caving with Greg

Don't you just hate it when you go to a new destination and end up not seeing or doing something you can see or do *only* in that place? Well, I've been through that and it still haunts me. Even though I spent a good two weeks in Meghalaya, I couldn't do the one thing that was on the top of my list – caving! Caving is basically an activity that involves using all your muscles and mind to stressfully squeeze, slip, slide, crawl and walk through a long underground passage. Yes, it's a lot of fun! Unfortunately, it rained the whole time I was there, and this is one adventure activity that you definitely cannot do in the rains of July. My friend Gobe, who did this once and loved it, teases me about it even now!

Gobe had gone to Shillong with a friend around five years ago and met a man called Greg, a famous caving instructor from the region. They call a cave 'krem' in Meghalaya. The Jaintia, Khasi and Garo Hills of the state are home to around 1,580 caves, out of which there are

980 caves that have been fully or partially explored by adventure lovers like Greg. The Krem Liat Prah holds the title of the longest cave in Meghalaya and the whole of India! It's 30,957 metres long!

Greg had planned a small caving expedition for Gobe and his friend, and it was going to be in a cave called Krem Mawmluh. This cave is located close to Cherrapunji, which is about 54 kilometres from Shillong. Gobe, his friend and Greg started the journey from Shillong early in the morning and reached the entrance of the cave in about an hour. Krem Mawmluh is a little over seven kilometres of cave passage, intersected in places by a shallow rivulet, which gets waist-deep in a few spots. But there was more to the entire thing than just going through a cave and crossing a waterbody…and Greg hadn't told them what to expect. It was a surprise! 'Are you up for a real adventure?' was all he'd asked, as they got out of the car.

The mouth of the cave was a 45-minute walk from the road through a grassy hill. Outside the cave, the three of them got into their gear. The gear included a wetsuit like the one you wear when you go diving (this keeps you warm inside), gum boots, a helmet for protection from the sharp edges of rocks, and the most important thing – a head light. The further you are away from the opening, the darker it gets.

They slowly started walking into the cave, Greg leading the way.

At first it was easy. They could walk straight into the opening and gaze up at the walls of Krem Mawmluh.

Stalagmites and stalactites rose up and hung from the floor and the ceiling. A stalagmite is a formation of calcium salts rising from the floor of a cave. The complete opposite formation is called a stalactite, which is made by dripping water. These make the caves look really creepy, but also quite fascinating. Gobe tells me that these were the biggest stalagmites and stalactites he had ever seen. 'They were gorgeous!' he said, his eyes shining. Greg even showed them small pools of water which had *blind* fish in them. They say that these fish never develop a sense of sight as they are born in complete darkness.

Soon the passage of the cave became narrower and one had to squeeze between rocks to get past. The ankle-length water had now reached their calves and it looked like it was only getting deeper. Eventually, they were waist-deep in water. This seemed a bit scary, but Gobe insisted that it was actually pretty exciting! The topography of the cave kept changing as they moved ahead and took different turns inside the cave. At one point they had to crawl on their bellies under a big rock or climb over a high one to get to the other side. When they had slipped, squeezed, crawled and climbed for more than two hours, Greg decided that it was time for them to turn and head back.

One has to be very, very careful and alert when inside a cave. There are sharp corners, rivulets and creatures one may not be used to (like the blind fish!), and some people can feel a bit suffocated. Now that they were familiar with the route, it took them lesser time to come back the same way. 'I wanted to be there for two more hours at least,' complained Gobe, when he was telling me about it. 'It was amazing. Fantastic! I definitely want to go again!' Obviously, he was doing nothing to make me feel less sad about missing the adventure. Hmpf.

How to Get to Shillong

Shillong doesn't have an airport within the city. The nearest well-connected airport to the hill station is in Guwahati in Assam, which is about 90 kilometres away. But it has a train station that is connected to other cities in India.

Other Caves in Meghalaya

- **Krem Dam:** This is close to a village called Mawsynram, the wettest place in India currently.
- **Mawsmai Cave:** Close to Cherrapunji, this cave has steps built inside.
- **Synrang-Pamiang:** This cave is 14,157 metres long and has amazing stalagmites and stalactites.
- **Siju:** This cave lies in the Garo Hills and also has beautiful formations.

Along the Alaknanda

I think the process of choosing holiday destinations always suffers from the Proximity Problem! All right, all right, it's a term I made up myself, but it makes complete sense. It means that if you live in a particular city, you never end up seeing the most beautiful places close to it, because you always feel, 'Oh, I can go there anytime. It's really right here! Let me explore something further off.' It happened to me with a lovely village called Jayalgarh, only 135 kilometres from my home in Dehradun. When I was growing up, my parents always felt it was 'too close' and it just kept getting pushed further and further down our list of 'must-visit places'. But this changed a few years ago.

The summers in Dehradun and the adjoining places like Rishikesh and Haridwar can get pretty warm, even if they are a good bit above sea level. The sun beats down with such force that roaming around in the afternoons gets quite difficult. The trees and bushes look droopy and exhausted, and even the birds hide themselves in the leaves until the sun decides to go home in the evenings. A couple of summers ago I was home for a week-long break from Bengaluru. The soaring temperatures were making my temper rise too, so I decided to get out and go on a short vacation. Google Maps came to the rescue as I scrolled, pinched and expanded my phone screen to see which destinations were close enough for a two-day break. That's when Jayalgarh popped up. It was perfect for a short, sweet and hopefully cool holiday.

The two-hour journey to Jayalgarh was dotted with glorious views of the green-tinged Ganga River hugging the deep gorges along the road. The river runs for kilometres through this region along the rocky mountains. I made only two stops – a short one at Rishikesh for a quick breakfast, and then another at Devprayag, where the rivers Alaknanda and Bhagirathi meet to make the Ganga. From here, my taxi swerved to the right, along the bubbling Alaknanda, for exactly 22 kilometres! Finally, a simple green board peeked out from behind a dense copse, and a row of white-topped tents emerged slowly. As I began to walk down the cobbly path leading to the campsite, I could already spot a few red rafts bobbing in and out of the river and a row of green loungers on the beach.

I soon sat down with a plate of yummy veggies (*saag* and cauliflower in a yoghurt curry) in one of the easy chairs in the dining area that was facing the river. The view from there was even more delicious than the food! The cook, Anmolji, who had stepped out of the kitchen to see if all the guests were eating well, told me about the significance of the Alaknanda River. The Alaknanda is one of the holiest rivers in India. It starts from the foot of the Satopanth and Bhagirath Kharak glaciers high up in the mountains, picks up silt along the way, becoming fatter and slimmer by turns in places, before finally reaching the plains.

The Alaknanda's rocky bed is known to create rapids that are great for rafting. The river twists and turns in parts, and rafting enthusiasts love navigating these sections. I had planned all my adventuring activities for the day after I arrived. On the first day, I just wanted to sit by the river and listen to stories. Before I knew it, the sun had sunk behind the mountains, leaving the sky with an orange tinge, which was soon swallowed up by the night sky. The sound of the river next to the camp must have worked like a lullaby, because I slept soundly that night.

The next day was completely different. There was a group staying at the camp that wanted to go rafting and needed one more person to make up the ideal weight on the raft. Let me tell you how rafting works. Around six people and an instructor sit on an inflatable boat (a raft) that can be steered with oars. Now this can work like a boat too, but the real fun is when you take it through really choppy waters of rivers, which are called rapids. The raft jumps up and dips down on these rapids, as it is extremely light, making it lots of fun for the people on it.

I happily joined the other travellers, and the camp team took us down to the beach from where we needed to board the rafts. The team helped us with our life jackets and other gear and introduced us to the instructor who would be with us for the two-hour-long experience.

We were going to cover the stretch from Jayalgarh to Devprayag, bouncing on Grade 2 and Grade 3 rapids. A Grade 1 rapid is the easiest, and Grade 5 is the toughest (read: scariest), so I was relieved to be somewhere in the middle! We were given a quick orientation by the guide, who was called Bahadur, on how to row with him, how to sit down when we were on the rapids, and finally how to save someone if they happened to spring out of the raft. The last tip made me shiver a little. What if I fell out? Looking at my worried face, Bahadur smiled and said, 'Don't worry, I'm here! I will jump in and save you. Besides, the life jacket will keep you afloat.'

Soon, we were off on the raft – six of us and Bahadur, the captain sitting right at the back. At first, the water was calm. Then there was a swift current, which made our raft glide over the water smoothly, but there were no rapids yet. We waved at the villagers working in their fields along the river and enjoyed the view of the bright blue sky and the mountainsides along our water highway.

Then came the first of the ten rapids. I was sitting on the top-right of the raft, and it was my responsibility to steer the raft with the oar, while the people sitting in the middle had to just sit tight. It was fun fighting the frothy rapids with the oar. We got out

of the rapid in only a few seconds, but it seemed much longer! Thankfully, there was someone *more* scared than me, whose shriek seemed to echo in the entire valley. (When we were in a rapid-less part, I asked her if she knew how to swim. 'Oh yes,' she answered, 'I used to swim for the state team!' I couldn't understand why she had yelled then!)

About two or three rapids later, I felt fairly confident and could understand Bahadur's instructions pretty well. After every successful crossing we all brought the oars together and cheered. The 25-kilometre stretch passed so quickly that I hardly realized when we'd reached almost the end of the trip. There was only one last rapid left to cross and no one had fallen off the raft yet. Brimming with confidence, off we went into the splashy water, the raft tumbling this way and that, Bahadur shouting over everyone about how we should row. This was a much longer rapid than the others, and I have to admit that I started feeling a little scared when the raft waddled up, dipped down and jumped back.

Luckily, we got out with everyone still on the raft, and we celebrated by banging our oars together! And then we floated towards a strip of sand along the river, where a jeep was waiting to take us back to Jayalgarh. Exhausted by all the rowing and the excitement, I snoozed off the moment I got in, only to be nudged awake by a grinning Bahadur, who was shouting, 'Get up, get up, the action isn't over!'

We reached a spot quite close to the camp at Jayalgarh, which had a rope bridge stretched across the river. Clearly, more adventures were lying in wait! It was time to try bridge crossing, hanging onto the rope like a monkey and clambering to the other side. Bahadur, who seemed to be an all-round adventurer, showed us how to do it and promised that the tightly strapped safety harness would make sure that nobody tumbled into the river. The fast-flowing river below still gave me the jitters. But then I decided that if I could brave rafting, I could brave this too! So, off I went – moving very, very slowly across the splashing river, my hands and legs wrapped around the rope. My short, sweet and cool holiday had turned into a full-blown adventure, but I loved it!

Now to tackle all the other places I'd ignored because of the Proximity Problem.

Getting to Jayalgarh

Jayalgarh is 111 kilometres from Jolly Grant Airport in Dehradun and 110 kilometres from the Haridwar railway station.

Fun at Jayalgarh

There are other things that can fill up your day besides hitting the water. Try your hand at rappelling through rocky outcrops, rock climbing, trekking, valley crossing, bridge slithering, cliff jumping and kayaking. Cliff jumping, by the way, involves diving straight into the water from a high rock!

Fly Like a Bird

When I was in Grade Four, I remember Mrs Nautiyal (we called her Ms Naughty, of course!) teaching us about phobias, and asking our class of 30 about the things that we were really scared of. The answers were varied. My classmates said things like 'fire', 'lizards', 'snakes', 'chillies', and so on. One even said, 'My father…gulp!'

I had none of those fears. Spiders? No problem! Cockroaches? Nah! Water? Umm, okay, a little bit, since I didn't know how to swim.

But when she asked if we were scared of *heights*, my hand shot up before anyone else.

When I was nine years old, the highest place that I had been to was the twentieth floor of my uncle's building in Delhi. I remember quite clearly how scary it was to peep down from the balcony! The only thing I liked about the balcony was being at eye level with the kites gliding about in slow-motion in the blue sky. I avoided looking down, though every now and then, when curiosity got the better of me, I'd take a quick peek, but the moment I saw the tiny ant-like people and vehicles down on the roads my heart would flutter in nervousness.

Over the years, however, it got better. I slowly overcame my fear of heights. I started looking down from my uncle's balcony for longer with my sister, making a game out of spotting familiar cars or people. I even developed a love for climbing trees – the taller, the better!

In fact, I find heights quite thrilling now. I've trekked to mountain peaks, climbed the Sydney Harbour Bridge, walked across a SUPER-high see-through glass bridge to cross a deep Canadian valley, gone parasailing in the Philippine ocean and zip-lined on 100-feet-high trees in New Zealand and not felt even an iota of fear.

The last thing I did that involved kite-level height was paragliding in Kumaon.

Last summer, my friend Vaibhav and I wanted to spend a quiet weekend away from Delhi, so we took off to Naukuchiatal, a serene lake in Uttarakhand. Kumaon is a hilly region in the state of Uttarakhand, and it is most famous for its beautiful valleys, the lakes sitting between them like cups of water and the snow-topped mountains that you can catch glimpses of as you go higher.

We found a lovely cottage with the loveliest view – of the greenish-blue Lake Naukuchiatal. Our holiday plan was simple – read, relax and drink many cups of tea, and let Goswamiji, the in-house cook, feed us every few hours. Anywhere else, I would have turned up my nose at the super-green veggies on my plate, but I'd never seen these greens before, and anything Goswamiji made seemed to be utterly delicious!

Our plan failed on the second day, because I decided that I was tired of all the relaxing that I'd done on the first day. My legs were a little *too* well rested and my brain a little *too* inactive. I needed to get out and do something. Walk around, go for a boat ride in the lake, or anything else that did not involve our bums staying sunk in chairs. I asked Goswamiji for some expert tips. He thought for a bit, then went rummaging around a drawer in his kitchen and finally came back with a leaflet.

It was an ad for paragliding in the hills very close to where we were. A quick phone call later, we were booked for a flight at noon.

Neither of us had ever done this before, so we wondered how it was going to be. Cold for sure. When you're flying high up, it gets pretty cool. The view would be excellent. We would naturally be flying tandem with an instructor. Tandem means alongside each other, or when something is done together by two people. In this kind of adventure activity, only a trained person can fly the paraglide. We would only have to sit tight, strapped to the glide. I got so excited talking about the flight that I had the two extra parathas that Goswamiji had sneaked into my plate without realizing it!

Soon, it was time to leave. We took a cab right up to the top of a hill, where there was a small lone shed with a red tin roof. There were three or four local instructors with the paragliding gear sitting inside. They were all set, ready to get us going. We started with a quick orientation – which was basically just a short talk by each of the instructors.

My instructor's name was Dawa. When I say Dawa's speech was short, I mean it was *really* short. It was literally three lines. *Hold on tight. This is the parachute buckle just in case. Enjoy the view.* He then carried a large parasail out into the open, attached it to the straps around me, checked a couple of times if everything was okay and asked me to get ready. 'Good luck!' I said to Vaibhav, who looked more nervous than me.

'Back towards me, face towards the hillside and run!' shouted Dawa.

I ran like a tortoise, with the heavy sail dragging behind me. Dawa kept his encouragement limited to only shouting, 'Faster, faster!'

I huffed and puffed and soon we were at the edge of the hill. Just as we reached, we went *whoooooooosh* into the valley. My organs must have shifted a bit as we dipped into the valley a fair amount. The instructor pulled something, tugged at something else and then we started rising up in a slow but steady way.

Oh, the sight was stunning! We were right among the clouds! Thank God I wore my jacket though, because the wind was C-H-I-L-L-Y. When we had steadied ourselves, Dawa finally spoke some more words. He told me that he had come from Nepal and that he loved flying with the birds like this. Dawa had taken over a thousand people on paragliding trips and was glad that I was not nervous. We chatted happily for a while. All was good, until Dawa asked me, 'Are you sure you're not nervous?'

I laughed. 'Absolutely not!'

'Will you be okay with some spinning then?'

'Sure,' I said, not knowing what he had in mind.

And off we went, legs up, heads down. Zipping down fast in circles. I felt like I'd been thrown into a washing machine! Soon, the ground got closer and closer. Houses and trees got bigger. I guess that meant we were landing. Just when we were getting too close for me to keep smiling, Dawa turned us back up and gently landed us in a field. Phew!

I'd had such a great time that I must have thanked Dawa a gazillion times. You must do this sometime when you're in Kumaon. But make sure you don't eat too many parathas before this.

How to Get to Naukuchiatal

The nearest railway station is in a small town called Kathgodam, which is 40 kilometres away. If you go from Delhi by road, the journey is about seven hours long.

Things to Do around Naukuchiatal

- **Bhimtal Lake:** Visit the more popular Bhimtal Lake, the largest lake in this region.
- **Mukteshwar:** Located 20 kilometres from Naukuchiatal, Mukteshwar is a small, beautiful town named after a 350-year-old temple called Mukteshwar Dham.
- **Birding:** If you're fond of birds, go walking in the mornings with a guide to spot hundreds of them. You should be able to see some of the common ones, like red-billed magpies, wood owls, Kalij pheasants, crested kingfishers and laughing thrushes.

Curious Careers

A Dentist with a Twist

Aaaaaa!'

'Eeeeee!'

'Aaaaaa!'

'Eeeeee!'

I turned this way and that but I just couldn't see the source of these sounds. I jumped a little bit every time I heard one of these scary noises, and despite the honking cars, whirring scooters and bikes, and rickshaw drivers zipping around as if they were driving racing cars, the sounds were loud and clear. I scratched my head in confusion till my friend Vaibhav, walking beside me, grinned and pointed to a small group of people sitting on the side of the road.

We were in Varanasi's Godowlia Chowk area, looking for a famous snack shop that served excellent chaat, sweets and savouries. The city is known for its busy markets and ancient temples. My focus, however, was solely on the yummy jalebis, barfis and other sweets that were soon going to go into my stomach. The Godowlia Chowk neighbourhood is located in the old part of the town along the Ganga River. It is crammed with temples and a buzzing market with hundreds of shops selling clothes, sweets, utensils, brass sculptures and more. There are even tongas (horse-drawn carts) that run from one end to another, ferrying devotees to the temples by the river.

While there was so much going on in the busy streets, this group squatting on the side of the road was far too interesting for us not to investigate further. We saw two women sitting on their haunches, mouths wide open, in front of an old man in saffron clothes. He peered into each mouth, knocked about inside with a metal tool to check the strength of their teeth and then either nodded or swung his head from side to side. 'Nah,' he said disapprovingly after looking at one woman's mouth. He then went on to take some more tools out of his bag and dug around her mouth again.

This kind of dental check-up was nothing like we had seen before, so we moved closer. The old man smiled as we approached and gestured for us to sit to his left so we could get a clear view of some yucky cavities, yellow teeth and their unhappy owners. We sat down and watched him gaze into those toothy mouths for another 20 minutes. Behind him was a small sign pasted on the wall, with huge dentures painted on it and the words 'Daanton ka Doctor' scribbled in Hindi below. A small table in front of the poster was packed with various metal tools, some white paste in a bowl and a dirty mug of water. The old man was a dentist, and this was his open-air clinic. No white coats, no whirring machines and no pills, but lots of dust and heat all around. I couldn't believe it – what a place to have a clinic!

One of the patients was a lady who complained of a rotting tooth that needed to be pulled out. The old man inspected her mouth again and turned to pick up a most ghastly looking object! It was a pair of pliers made of iron. He promptly put it in the lady's mouth, got a grip on the tooth creating the problem and yanked it clean out of her mouth. I swear his arm swung right back with the tooth clasped between the pliers! The lady held her mouth in pain while screaming, 'Aaaaaa!' She looked away and spat out a litte bit of blood onto the dusty street. A minute later, after feeling the inside of her mouth with her tongue, she smiled with satisfaction. The tooth was gone!

When, finally, the saffron-robed man was done, we managed to have a quick chat with him to find out more about this unique dental clinic by the road. His name was Ram Babaji, and he'd been a dentist in this very spot for nearly 30 years! What a long time! And before him, his father and his grandfather had been dentists in the *exact same spot*. Ramji had never studied anything about teeth – in fact, he had dropped out of school pretty early – but he'd learnt all about them from his father, who, in turn, had learnt from his father.

'So, no studies? No going to college to learn about teeth?' I asked curiously.

He waved my questions away like they were an annoying fly.

'What about germs?' I tried again.

Ramji was convinced that the overly clean city clinics were just making too much of a fuss over nothing. Teeth were simple to understand. If they had gone bad, they had to be yanked out, and if they were ugly or crooked, they *still* had to be yanked out.

When we asked him about using painkillers, gloves and clean equipment, he just laughed. 'All that is for wimps!' He pointed to the white paste behind him and demonstrated how he made dentures with it. People have been coming to him for years and trusted him to get their teeth problems solved. Well, I guess that explained the long queues for his treatment!

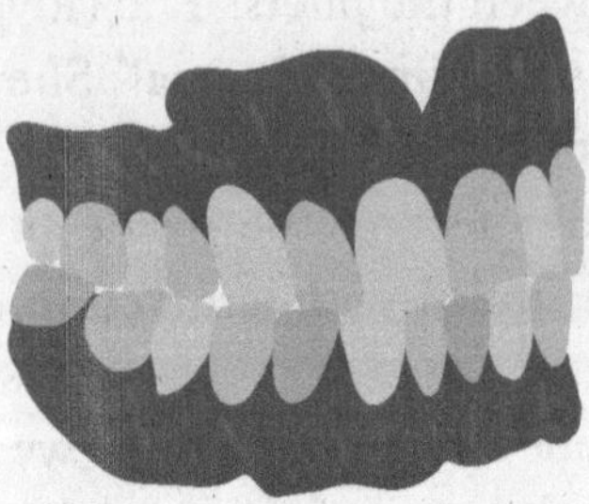

All through talking to us, Ram Babaji kept chewing paan, and we watched his lips slowly turn from orange to red. After our chat was over, we asked if we could take a photograph of him. When Vaibhav asked him to smile, he refused. After much prodding and requesting, Ram Babaji finally gave us a wide grin. There were no surprises there – most of his teeth had fallen out, and the ones that remained looked shaky enough to fall off any time! I couldn't help but ask how he was a dentist when his own teeth weren't in the best shape.

'Arre,' he answered, clearly irritated, 'because my own teeth are so bad, I know exactly what my patients are going through. And you see all these gaps?' He pointed to the many spaces between his few teeth. 'I pulled them out myself.'

We finally got up to find our way to our original destination – the famous sweet shop. Ram Babaji waved and said, 'Don't worry, even if you eat too many sweets and your teeth go bad, you can always come to me!'

Vaibhav and I looked at each other in horror and decided to give up finding the shop.

Reaching Varanasi

Being an important city for pilgrimages, there are many flights and trains that connect major Indian cities to Varanasi. Godowlia Chowk is in the heart of the old part of Varanasi. The neighbourhood is located in the middle of the spiritual action and has hundreds of small and big temples that lie on the banks of the Ganga.

How Not to Have Your Teeth Pulled Out by Ram Babaji

If you don't want to keep visiting your dentist, here's a great way to keep your teeth healthy

Step 1: Always brush twice a day – in the morning and before going to bed.

Step 2: Brush lengthwise along your teeth.

Step 3: Clean your tongue with a tongue cleaner.

Step 4: Don't eat too many chocolates and sweets – I know it's difficult, but try!

Step 5: Use floss to get rid of food stuck between your teeth.

Tikam Chand and His Trusty Camera

I don't know about you, but I *hate* being in photographs with a straight face! I love sticking my tongue out, closing my eyes tightly or scrunching up my nose. This, as I'm sure you can tell, usually annoys the person behind the camera no end, but I love it! Even if the photograph comes out badly, you can always take it again and again until you get one you like, right?

But did you know that before the year 1990, you couldn't simply *keep* taking photos without a care in the world? You see, it was only after 1990 that digital cameras were introduced to us. Before this, still or film cameras were used to take photographs, and there was *no way* to look at the image immediately after clicking it. You couldn't take another picture if the lighting wasn't right, or if everyone wasn't smiling properly or if someone had moved. The photograph was captured on a film or plate and then developed in a dark room using chemicals. There was never any telling how the photograph may come out. While this was a lot of fun, it was also very frustrating! And expensive, as one had to get the right paper and the correct chemicals and build a dark room to develop the photographs. So much effort! So much money!

If we go further back in time from 1990 (and even *I* don't remember that time), the cameras were HUGE. They were big and boxy and came with a thousand attachments and lenses – they certainly couldn't be carried around on holidays as easily as today's cameras. If you wanted to be photographed, you would have to stand EXTREMELY still and wait for *days* to see the final result. I don't think I could have managed to be still at all. You know how much I like moving about and making funny faces! The photographer would have been quite angry with me!

Speaking of photographs, there's one man in Jaipur who loves vintage cameras and has devoted his life to taking pictures with a massive, bulky one, making sure that people appreciate the effort that went into taking a picture in the good old days. Boy, he must be very patient with his subjects, waiting for them to be absolutely still so he can get a perfect shot.

A few years ago, I was visiting Jaipur and decided to stroll around the old city. The buildings in this part of town are all reddish pink, giving Jaipur the name it is known by across the world – the Pink City. I was roaming around a palace called Hawa Mahal, and was so busy admiring the beautiful old buildings and the bustling market that I didn't see a big black object, almost as tall as me, propped up on three legs, and a man bending behind it, a large black cloth covering both him and this strange thing. *Wham!* Even after we collided, I could only see a pair of legs sticking out from behind the black cloth (accompanied by a muffled groan).

I immediately apologized to this strange apparition and waited for someone to appear from behind the cloth.

Finally, a moustached man emerged, visibly frustrated (oops!) but managing to smile a little because I had apologized profusely. He introduced himself as Tikam Chand and explained that it was difficult to redo the kind of photographs he was taking and that he needed to be very still. That's when I realized that the big black object was a *camera* and that he'd been taking a *picture*. His hapless subjects, a man and his wife, standing a little farther away (I hadn't noticed them earlier! Oops!), would have to act like statues all over again. I said I was sorry to the whole group, but I hung around to see how this weird method of taking photos actually worked.

After giving the couple some instructions, Tikam Chand disappeared below the cloth. A split second later, their smiles were frozen in place, there was no movement whatsoever and out came a muffled voice from below the cloth, 'Okayyy, done!'

Tikam Chand then came out of his black hideout, took out a piece of paper from the camera and dipped it in a bucket of water. 20, 30, 40, 60 seconds later, the couple's photograph emerged on the paper – just like magic! He looked at the paper and grinned widely. It was a perfect photo!

After his clients left, Tikam Chand and I sat down with a cup of tea each near his camera. I wanted to know why he was still taking pictures in this very old way. Cameras have become so easy to use, so I was surprised that Tikam had decided to stick with an old one. Now we can adjust the light, take multiple photos quickly and change filters or colours. Tikam must really love the old style of photography! He took a long sip of his tea, *sluuuurp*, and told me his story.

Even as a young child, Tikam was interested in how cameras worked. This was long before digital cameras or smartphones had even been thought of, much less invented! His inspiration was his grandfather, Pahari Master, who was employed by the king of Jaipur to take photographs of the royal family. Tikam Chand used to watch his grandfather disappear behind the black cloth of the full-frame camera (that's what these big cameras are called), adjust the lens in the front and then meticulously alter the settings as per the light outside. Then, he would dig into the wooden box, fiddle around with his arms inside the legs of a pair of denim jeans and pull out a white sheet of paper to dip in a pail of water next to him. Slowly, a black-and-white photograph would appear on the paper. This fascinating method stuck in Tikam's head and, learning by watching, he was able to replicate this process even in his grandfather's absence.

In the year 1977, Tikam finally dusted off his grandfather's old camera, propped it upright on a tripod with the help of bricks and opened a shop for anyone who wanted their photograph in black and white. It worked quite differently. This was a Polaroid camera, in which images would get printed on paper. It had a film (a strip of plasticky paper) at the back of the camera, on which the image would be captured. Today, we have digital sensors instead of the film.

In the beginning, his customers were mainly locals who wanted to document an important occasion – birthdays, anniversaries and other such happy moments. Then, Tikam Chand decided to share this unique way of taking pictures with people from all over the world. And the best place to do that was right in the heart of the old city, where there would be a lot of Indian and foreign travellers.

Soon enough, people were intrigued by this strange object and its moustached owner and were only too eager to sit on a stool and act like statues. And watch their photograph emerge on paper. Happy travellers would pay up to ₹100 for each picture. Earlier this was a great business for Tikam Chand. All the materials – the film, the chemicals and the spare parts – were easily available. They were not expensive and he could concentrate on his photography without worrying. But life is a little tough for Tikam Chand now, as

the chemicals and the photo paper for his camera are not readily available in India anymore. He needs to get them from France and pays a heavy price for it. But Tikam Chand doesn't want to give up taking pictures this way unless he absolutely has to. He loves this vintage style of photography too much. 'I don't want the craft to die,' he said. He even encouraged me to sit on the stool and have my photo taken so that I would always remember him.

But as usual, I could hardly sit still. I made a funny face and all that came out of Tikam Chand's magic box was a blur!

How to Reach Jaipur and Tikam Chand

Jaipur is the capital of Rajasthan, so you can easily get to the city by train, flight or car. Once you're in the city, head towards the famous Hawa Mahal area. To the right of Hawa Mahal, sandwiched between clothing stores, is where Tikam Chand sets up his makeshift photo stall. You can identity it because of the large black camera standing on a tripod and Tikam's head, which is mostly covered under a large black cloth behind it. He sits here every day from 11 a.m. to 6 p.m.

Places to See around Tikam Chand's Shop

Hawa Mahal: Meaning 'the palace of the winds', Hawa Mahal is made of red and pink sandstone and is known for its beautiful windows.

Isar Lat: Also known as Swargasuli, Isar Lat is a seven-storey tower built by Sawai Ishwari Singh (a raja of the Amber kingdom) after he won a war. You can see the entire city from here.

City Palace: One of the mains sights in the city, this is the royal palace of Jaipur's king.

Jantar Mantar: This observatory is home to a collection of 19 massive astronomical instruments, including the world's largest sundial, and was built by the Rajput king Sawai Jai Singh II.

Turban Museum of Jaipur: Housed in a restaurant, the turban museum showcases the bright and colourful turbans worn by men from different tribes in the state.

The Dabbawalas of Mumbai

Does your stomach make crazy sounds when you're hungry? Something that sounds like this – *groooowwwwwwl*? Well, mine roars like a tiger when it wants food.

I thought my growl was the loudest till I bumped into my neighbour Mr Pednekar at a grocery shop close to lunchtime one day. We had just said 'Hi!' when, all of a sudden, his stomach made such a loud noise that I almost jumped. He smiled sheepishly and apologized for startling me. He explained that he was a lousy cook, and his wife had many other things to take care of that day, which was why lunch was still not ready. He had wandered off for a walk to distract himself and had come to the shops for a quick snack.

We started walking back to our apartment building together, him devouring a packet of biscuits (and not sharing even one with me – *humpf!*). In the middle of crunching a biscuit, Mr Pednekar told me that he could not deal with hunger at all – especially when he was at work. Any time a meal got delayed, he'd feel faint and his stomach would make horrendous sounds in protest. Of course, this can be very embarrassing at office, and that's why he relied on the trusted *dabbawalas* of Mumbai to ensure that his lunch came on time.

Mumbai's *dabbawalas* are a team of more than 5,000 men whose job is to pick up more than two lakh lunch boxes from homes or restaurants across the city, deliver them to people in offices and exchange the empty boxes for full ones the next day. They dress in crisp white kurta-pyjamas, wear Gandhi caps and are always on time. *Always.* In fact they're better at timekeeping than your watch! Their work is tough because Mumbai is such a huge city, and the distances between places can take hours to navigate. Besides, there are constant traffic jams that bring everything to a halt on the roads. The *dabbawalas* also have to account for delays from homes and restaurants, but they never let their customers down.

This food delivery service is more than 100 years old (much older than Swiggy and Zomato!), and it was started by a man called Mahadeo Havaji Bachche in 1890. Since then, the efficient and organized team has grown to thousands of men and has spread to all the different corners of the city.

Mr Pednekar's packet of biscuits was almost half over and so was our walk home. I asked him if he knew how the *dabbawalas* coordinated between each other, the different

colours and sizes of lunch boxes, office addresses and the *exact* people they needed to deliver to. Mr Pednekar had been using this service for the past 25 years, so he knew exactly how it worked. He told me that the *dabbawala*s had come up with a method to make sure that nothing went wrong, ever.

First, a *dabbawala* goes around a neighbourhood on a bicycle, collecting all the tiffin boxes that need to be taken to different offices from homes and restaurants. He then delivers this set of boxes to a collection-and-sorting point at the nearest railway station. Here, different colours and symbols are put on the boxes to allocate them to different destinations. Then, these boxes are put in train coaches heading for different locations in the city. A special delivery coach in every train is reserved for the hundreds of boxes that need to get to hungry clients. Mumbai is HUGE, so this is the fastest way to reach every office in time for lunch. At each station, the *dabba*s of that location are handed to a local *dabbawala*, who then jumps on a bicycle to deliver them to different offices. Since he is on a bicycle, he can reach people faster than if he used a car or a motorcycle, because he can avoid traffic jams. Besides, bicycles are an affordable way for the *dabbawalla*s to get around.

And so, just before lunchtime, you'll see scores of men in white kurta-pyjamas flitting between offices, making their deliveries to satisfied customers. They are in such a rush that there is no time to stop and say hi to another team member or take a chai break. It is said that the *dabbawalas* make only one mistake in every six million deliveries. That's a pretty awesome track record!

Mr Pednekar also told me that most of the *dabbawalas* come from a village near Pune and are often related to each other. While they work from Monday to Saturday each week, they do take an annual holiday for four days in March for a local festival in their village. The service is stopped during this period. Just talking about this prospective break in his tiffin schedule made Mr Pednekar look nervous – it certainly seemed like the worst time of the year for him!

Meeting the Dabbawalas of Mumbai

Head to Churchgate Station or Chhatrapati Shivaji Maharaj Terminus (popularly known as CST) around noon to see the *dabbawalas* of South Mumbai bring down lunch boxes, load them into carts and get them out for delivery.

Places to See Near Churchgate and CST

- **Rajabai Clock Tower**: This tower was designed by Sir George Gilbert Scott, who modelled it on the Big Ben in London.
- **Sassoon Docks**: These docks are some of the oldest harbours in Mumbai.
- **Flora Fountain**: A large fountain surrounded by second-hand bookshops with heaps of books lined up like tall towers, this is one of Mumbai's best-known landmarks.
- **Chowpatty Beach**: It may not be the cleanest beach you've seen, but it has lots of snack shops for a quick and delicious bite.
- **Mani Bhavan**: This is a lesser-known museum and library dedicated to Mahatma Gandhi. You'll find it in South Mumbai.

Babu Khan's Legacy

It was a clear day in Jaipur. There were no clouds at all – just a perfect blue sky. But it was ablaze with a riot of colours. At least 20 kites – pink, red, green and yellow – swayed softly in the afternoon breeze, sometimes darting sharply towards one another to cut the other's string. A pink kite was the only calamity I saw, though – it was cut swiftly by a green one. The defeated pink one immediately came floating down, most likely on top of one of the houses in the distance.

I decided to trace the owner of a blue kite along the string it was on.

A few hours earlier, I had arrived at the beautiful Jal Mahal Palace in the city, which is built in the middle of the sparkling waters of the Man Sagar Lake, giving visitors a great background for selfies. The lovely ochre structure and its reflection in the water look so peaceful and serene that one could easily mistake the sight for a gigantic painting! It's only when the black cormorants, white herons and spot-billed ducks decide to take short flights around the palace or dive into the water to catch fish, making the water ripple, that you can see some movement.

Located just behind this amazing lake is a large, dusty, grassless ground called the Karbala. It is surrounded by crumbling houses, and many garbage mounds lie around the makeshift cricket pitch in the middle. What a contrast to the tranquil waterbody! But if you like being in the middle of action rather than in a calm environment (like me!), then you might find the Karbala more fun! Despite the blazing heat of the afternoon, the field always buzzes with activity. You will be welcomed by the sound of a roaring '*Ouuuutttt!*' long before you put a single foot on this dusty expanse. A troop of excited cricket players occupies this space the whole day, and they leave only when the sun dips and it's difficult to see the ball any more.

But I was looking for someone else. When I finally spotted who was flying the blue kite – a happy old man – I was standing at the mouth of the field, just where the ball had rolled in for a four. I picked up the ball to fling it back to the closest fielder and asked if the men in the corner were professional kite fliers. The sweaty, sunburnt young fielder nodded and ran back to the pitch. The men didn't see me coming because they were busy looking at the cloudless sky, shading their eyes with their hands, necks craned upwards. Their gaze only dropped when I said 'Namaste!'; they were surprised to find out that I had travelled to Jaipur especially to look for a *patang dangal* (kite playground) and its keepers.

When I was younger, I loved seeing kites flying high but was never able to learn how to get one up in the air and make it sway in the wind. I must have tried a thousand times. After many years, when I found out that some people actually took kite-flying as a serious sport, I was curious to learn more about them.

Jaipur has been the centre for kite-flying in India for many, many years. Every year, 14 January is celebrated as Makar Sankranti in a number of Indian states. The festival marks the end of winter and welcomes the longer days of spring. Kite-flying, eating sweets, dancing and singing are part of the festivities. Jaipur celebrates with great enthusiasm, and that's why people love flying kites here. They take it quite seriously, learning how to fly one for months, buying lots of colourful kites on the day of Makar Sankranti and having regular competitions through the year.

I had a truckload of questions for this group. Were they a group of regulars? How many clubs were there in Jaipur? How many people were in each club? When did they practise? Did they hold competitions? Were these competitions annual? Which was the biggest championship? And which one of them possessed Babu Khan's kites? The last question brought a smile to several faces.

Hearing 'Babu Khan', the oldest gentleman, Rafiq, sat on the ground. Close to his feet lay a few large, flat, squarish suitcases in which were contained their most prized possessions – kites. He flipped open his suitcase and the label 'Babu Khan' peered up at me. We all bent down on our haunches and inspected the artistry of not one but about ten handmade kites, each of a unique design.

Spotting us peering at something on the ground as if there was a great treasure there, some boys even left their nail-biting cricket game midway and joined us.

Rafiq spoke passionately about the master craftsman. Appreciation poured in from others in the group as well. Most of the older men had flown kites with Babu Khan and missed his company. Sadly, Khan had died in 2014 at the age of 76.

Babu Khan had started flying kites at an early age like any other young boy in his village. He loved how the kites fluttered at first and then went higher and higher, till they looked like they were talking to the clouds. He practised hard and became one of the best kite fliers of his neighbourhood. Not only was he one of the most skilled fliers around, but he was also an excellent kite-maker! He used a special method of pasting different coloured papers together to make a smooth base, instead of just drawing on the kite. This is called appliqué work. When he was old enough, Babu Khan started participating in kite-flying competitions, winning most of them.

Rafiq then moved on to telling me about the different sizes that kites come in and other specifics. The strings were specifically sourced from Bareilly. Rafiq's group included about 150–200 people in Jaipur. These were serious hobbyists who'd formed over 12 teams that fought each other in the annual

competition during Makar Sankranti. They ran local shops and businesses. When there were no competitions, they practised in the afternoons when business in their shops was slow. The daily duels are known as *dangal.*

As I was beginning to understand the finer details of kite-flying, someone spotted Feroze, Babu Khan's grandson, and called him over. When he heard about the purpose of my visit, he immediately offered to take me home, where his grandfather's legendary kites were kept very carefully in steel boxes. I hopped onto Feroze's motorcycle, and we zipped through the snaking lanes behind the Karbala, avoiding stubborn cows who were policing the streets.

Soon, we reached Feroze's home, and large steel boxes were pulled out from under the bed. Each kite crafted by Babu Khan had been preserved in a sealed plastic cover. I was terrified of damaging them, so I asked Feroze to hold them up for me to see. Birds, cartoons, Mahatma Gandhi, various Hindu gods, the Taj Mahal, Medina and other Indian motifs decorated the wafer-thin paper. Babu Khan's delicate appliqué work was particularly famous.

Feroze pointed to a photograph I had seen in several articles about his famous grandfather – Babu Khan expertly handling a string with a hundred kites on it! It was the biggest draw for onlookers, who'd come to see Khan showcase his kite-flying talent. He was one of the finest kite-makers and fliers of the country, who'd travelled all over the world, to places like the USA, Taiwan, London and New Zealand, for kite-flying festivals. But he is best remembered for the time he managed to fly 500 kites on a single string in Goa in 2004. What a sight that must have been!

How to Get to Jaipur

Jaipur is well connected to major cities and towns of India. To find the Karbala ground, you'll have to go to the Jal Mahal Palace and walk to its right.

Have You Tried Making Your Own Kite?

Here's what you'll need: a plastic sheet (you can make this out of a polybag – this is a good way of reusing plastic that would otherwise be in a landfill), string, two sticks and ribbons.

Step 1: Cut the plastic bag into the shape of a kite (diamond).

Step 2: Paste the sticks along the length and breadth of the cut-out.

Step 3: Connect the ends of the sticks with a string.

Step 4: Attach the ribbons to the bottom.

Step 5: Tie a long string to the base of the kite.

Step 6: Find a terrace to fly your kite!

Marvellous Monuments

Dining with the Dead

Ever noticed how the telling of a ghost story is usually reserved for evenings? Preferably around a crackling bonfire, everyone's faces lit by the orange flames. Or surrounded by misty, cold mountains, the clouds filling up the valleys with shadows and the wind making eerie sounds. When the surroundings are sufficiently spooky, even the smallest rustling noise can make you jump a foot into the air!

But my story is slightly different. It was a bright, sunny morning, and the large black hands of the white clock on the wall showed a cheerful 8 a.m. I was sitting in a bustling market in Ahmedabad with my guide, Pramodbhai. We had met for breakfast at New Lucky Restaurant at Lal Darwaja so we could explore the old part of the city that day. The old part of town is a busy and fascinating neighbourhood with incredible architecture, ranging from centuries-old mosques and mausoleums to heritage hotels and crumbling homes. The slim lanes in the market are crammed with shops selling all sorts of things – food, clothes, utensils, toys – you name it, it's there. I was particularly interested (as usual) in the famous snack shops (Ahmedabad is known for them) and the ancient mosques. A big breakfast was needed before starting a long day of strolling around. Pramodbhai was slurping his chai loudly from a white ceramic saucer instead of from his teacup, and I was waiting patiently for my bun and jam combo.

What's that? What's so spooky about this story, you ask? Hang on to your pants, won't you? I've only just started this tale!

I had lots of questions for Pramodbhai about the different mosques and monuments of Lal Darwaja and the bustling street food scene. He told me the legend of Sidi Sayyed from Ethiopia, who'd built a mosque close to where New Lucky Restaurant is and the Bhadra Fort, which was a surveying point during Sultan Ahmed Shah's reign. Both were on our walking trail. We were also going to visit the Akhand Jyot, a lamp placed in a hole in the nearby Teen Darwaja. This lamp has apparently been burning for six hundred years! It was going to be an exciting day. When I paused between my seemingly never-ending queries, Pramodbhai gave me a slight smile and asked, 'Do you want to know a story about something more interesting than all the kings and their mosques?'

I nodded excitedly. Of course I did!

Sitting across from me, his head bent to take sips of his tea, Pramodbhai began to tell me about his encounters with a lady in a white sari, who only appeared at midnight at the junction close to the restaurant. Every time he crossed the junction after 11 p.m., she would float in mid-air in front of his rusty old once-green scooter, grinning widely and holding out her hand as if to ask for a lift. She was said to be the ghost of a woman who had once lived nearby and died more than 70 years ago.

'The first time I saw her drifting towards me, I nearly ran into a pole. And a few times after that, the sight of her made me break into a cold sweat. But now I'm used to her. I sometimes even miss her when she doesn't appear,' he said proudly, seeming rather brave compared to how I was feeling. Just imagining a white-sari-clad woman floating in front of me, trying to get a lift, gave me goosebumps. But that wasn't all – Pramodbhai had one incident after another to narrate! Apparently, on one occasion, she had tried to hop on to his scooter as a pillion rider. Another time, she had called out his name. And yet another time, he swore he had seen two of her come at him together.

A chill ran down my spine – not because I wasn't used to ghost stories, but because we were sitting right in the middle of two graves. As it turns out, New Lucky Restaurant is a unique place where the dead are really all *around* you. The restaurant was built on what was once a graveyard hundreds of years ago, with tombstones scattered all over the place.

When the city expanded and this land was given out for buildings to be made, one particular section with 12 tombstones landed up with Mr Krishnan Kutti, the owner.

He thought long and hard about building a restaurant right on top of a cemetery. What would happen to the tombstones? How disrespectful it would be to erase them! After much thinking, he decided that the folks who had died could just continue to be around those who were alive and kicking. He built the walls of the restaurant and the kitchen, and he arranged the furniture around the tombstones. In fact, as a mark of respect, he even has his staff clean the tombstones every morning, cover them with green shrouds and place flowers on them.

No one really knows whom these tombstones belong to, and some claim they are at least 300 years old. It suddenly occurred to me that one of them could be the home of Pramodbhai's friend in the white sari – and I promptly shuddered in fear!

Once he was done with his tale, Pramodbhai slurped up one more tea in complete silence, looking at me in between sips to see if I was scared enough. I must have had beads of sweat dotting my forehead. Pramodbhai stifled a giggle seeing my pale face. Then, his face contorted, trying to control a guffaw, but in a matter of seconds, the little snorts had turned into full-blown laughter. Clearly, he had been joking all this while about the white-sari lady, just to see how I'd react. I could have cheerfully strangled him, but I decided to laugh instead.

While the made-up story about the woman in the white sari was one that Pramodbhai told all his clients at the start of each tour, it was true that the graves had been there for years. I wonder why Mr Kutti named the restaurant New Lucky instead of The Graveyard. I think it was probably because the company of the dead brought him lots of luck. You see, the restaurant was packed by the time we left.

Getting to New Lucky Restaurant

New Lucky Restaurant is located in in the old neighbourhood of Lal Darwaja and opposite City College in Ahmedabad. Ahmedabad is very well connected by flights, trains and buses to major cities across India.

By the way, apart from the grave and M.F. Husain's painting (see the next page), the Pineapple Maska Bun here is also quite famous. I would recommend it with a cup of hot and sweet tea or a milkshake!

Discover Amazing Ahmedabad

- **The M.F. Husain Painting**: Along with the graves, New Lucky Restaurant is also home to a painting by the famous artist M.F. Husain, who left a painting worth lakhs for the owner. You can still see it hanging on one of the walls.
- **Sabarmati Ashram**: This place on the banks of the Sabarmati was home to Mahatma Gandhi from 1917 to 1930. It's where he started the Dandi March to protest against the British tax on salt.
- **Auto World Vintage Car Museum**: You can see an excellent collection of over 100 vintage cars here.
- **Adalaj ni Vav**: Explore this beautiful well that has steps that you can take to walk down till you reach the water.
- **Sidi Bashir Mosque**: Go here to see an old mosque with two minarets that sway, but never fall, when shaken!

The Charm of Charminar

It's a sea of heads in front of you, bobbing up and down, moving from side to side. What's that, you ask? Well, that's all you can see as you walk around the bustling old city in Hyderabad on a weekend. The streets are busy with eager shoppers and people going to one of the oldest mosques in town or crowding at the best biryani restaurants.

If you look away from the vastly varied hairstyles and hairlines in front of you, you'll also see rows and rows of shops selling pearls, attar (perfumes sold in small glass bottles), veggies, clothes, bangles, furniture, books, curios, toys, sweets, utensils, poultry, naan... The list goes on and on! Far in the distance stands a tall structure with a minaret in each of its corners, looming over the rest of the market. This is the Charminar (which literally means 'four pillars').

The Charminar is undoubtedly the most famous structure in Hyderabad, and it stands in the middle of the old city, narrow streets expanding outwards from its base in all directions. To me, it feels like a beehive, because the streets are always buzzing with people here!

Some time ago, I was walking down one of the main streets leading up to the monument. But before I could explore it to my heart's content, there was one thing I absolutely needed to do.

My mother had given me strict instructions to buy her a string of pearls from Mangatrai Pearls. This is the oldest shop for pearls in the town, and my mother was clear about wanting it from that shop only. 'Please don't go to any of the new shops!' she had said, wagging a finger at me.

So there I was, being swept along by the people thronging near the Charminar, in search of Mangatrai's, which had apparently been in the same place since 1935.

Soon, I found myself standing in front of this old and dazzling shop filled with all kinds of pearls. While I was going through what seemed like millions of designs, sizes and types of pearls, the salesperson chatted merrily about how busy the Charminar area had become over the years. I smiled and agreed, telling him that all I could see were the backs of people's heads. He laughed and said, 'Why don't you climb the Charminar? Then you'll only see the tops of their heads!' Well, that was exactly where I was headed!

Getting out of Mangatrai, dodging hawkers and braving the crowds, I finally reached the entry to Charminar, only to be surrounded by a number of guides clamouring to show me around. They all promised me fascinating stories, a proper insight into the history of the monument and the area and plenty of anecdotes. It was finally Aslam, with his greying beard, a wise, kind expression and a low, pleasant voice, who became my accomplice for the afternoon. We bought our tickets and joined a long queue meandering up to the top of the structure. A lightless winding staircase is the only way to get to the top, and I have got to tell you that it gets a little stuffy; and sweat, chatter and, the worst of all, a smelly fart, can really spoil the climb for the rest! Thankfully, the steps open up to the four airy corridors adjoining the four minarets. You can walk here and look down at the amazing view.

Aslam had started telling me the story of the Charminar area right from the base, so by the time we reached the gallery that joins the minarets, he could show me the other historic buildings nearby and the action in the markets. He told me that Charminar was built in 1591 as a mosque by a ruler called Muhammad Quli Qutb Shah. Some say that it was constructed to mark the middle of the city, and some say it was commissioned to celebrate the eradication of the deadly disease cholera. I decided to go with another story – that it was built by Quli Qutb Shah for his wife, Baghmati, whom he had first laid eyes on at that exact spot and fallen in love with instantly.

Quli Qutb Shah is said to have invited Persian architects to suggest designs and improvements for the structure when it was being built. Soft arches and nature motifs were the main design features of the minarets, which were built on lotus-leaf bases, a motif used in many Qutb Shahi buildings. The minarets are still intact, though a few silly people have scribbled and scratched their names on different walls of the entire structure. What a very idiotic thing to do to such an important structure!

Our slow, snaking queue finally reached the top, from where we had a bird's eye view of the entire area. It was a stunning sight – and a great relief to not be in the middle of the crush. I could see that there were four main streets on each side of the Charminar. Aslam told me their names – Patthargatti was the broadest, with shops selling clothes, perfumes, yummy biryani and Hyderabad's famous pearls. This was the street I had walked down. Then there was Laad Bazaar on the western side, dotted with sparkling bangle shops. I could also see items for wedding ceremonies and rich fabrics on this street. Rathkhana Street was relatively low-key, eventually leading up to many naan shops. The fourth street was the Charminar Road, which had a really interesting mosque close to where we were standing. This was the Makkah Masjid. I could see that the beautiful mosque had a wide courtyard with more pigeons than people! Aslam told me that the bricks of the main arch of this 17th-century mosque were made from the soil of Mecca, the holiest place in the world for Muslims.

We spent another half an hour spotting famous bakeries and restaurants, and Aslam also pointed out all the other famous monuments close by. I found the story of Golconda Fort particularly interesting. This was the main fort of the Qutb Shahi dynasty, and it was built close to the diamond mines, which are about ten kilometres from here. It is said that Charminar was connected to Golconda by an underground tunnel. But since no one had actually seen it, one can't tell if it's simply a rumour or the truth.

Aslam and I finally walked down the steps to the base of the structure again and strolled to the Nimrah Bakery, an Iranian café that we had seen from the top of the minar. Aslam promised me that a cup of tea and their signature Osmania biscuits would be even better than the view from the Charminar! The bakery was opened only in 1993, but the owner, Mr Abood bin Aslam al Katheri, has been a master baker since 1967. Our tea arrived in white ceramic teacups with two biscuits placed on the saucer. I bit into a biscuit and found that Aslam was absolutely right. The soft, crumbly thing melted in my mouth – I had never had such delicious biscuits before! It seemed silly to stop at just two; Aslam and I finished at least ten each. 'These biscuits are the real treasure of the Charminar area, and not the pearls that I had come looking for,' I told him while leaving for my hotel.

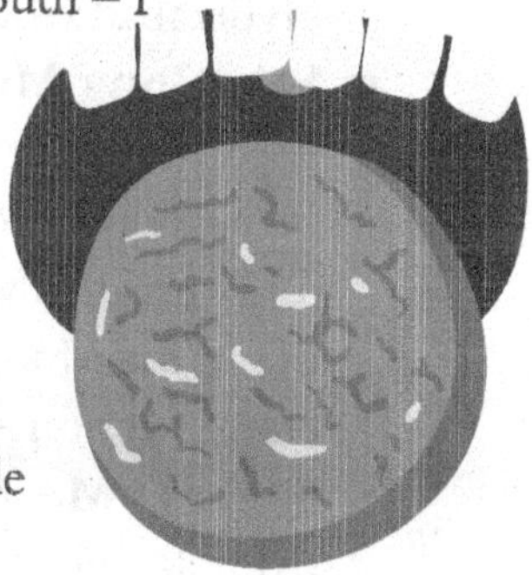

How to Get to Charminar

Hyderabad is well connected by flights, trains and buses to all major cities in India. If you're not staying in the old city, take a cab or an auto to this area. 'Let's go to the Charminar!' is all you need to say.

Sights around the Charminar

- **Makkah Masjid:** This is one of the largest mosques in India and can seat more than 20,000 people at one time.
- **Chowmahalla Palace:** This was once said to be the official residence of the Nizams of Hyderabad while they ruled the Hyderabad state.
- **Salar Jung Museum:** A sprawling art museum with sculptures, paintings, carvings, textiles, manuscripts, ceramics, carpets, clocks and furniture, this was once the private art collection of the Salar Jung family. Be sure to check out the clocks section – it's my favourite!
- **Nizam Museum:** This is a museum that exhibits only the gifts received by the last Nizam of Hyderabad, Osman Ali Khan, Asaf Jah VII, received on his silver jubilee. Imagine having a museum only for your gifts!
- **Golconda Fort:** Located a short drive away from Charminar, this is a fascinating erstwhile citadel close to the famous Golconda diamond mines.

The Thar Desert Museum

Do you like museums? I can't really make up my mind about them. I find some parts of a museum really fun and interesting, and some others so boring that I feel like I'm sleepwalking (especially if they are filled with exhibits of old manuscripts from hundreds of years ago)! But do you know which section makes me yawn the very second I walk into the room? The household objects one. And this is at *every single* museum I have ever been to! I *hate* gazing at pots and pans. But I absolutely love the clothes and jewellery section. What bright colours, what exquisite garments! What delicately embroidered fabrics! It really is fun to see what people wore in another time and age.

On my last trip to the town of Jodhpur in Rajasthan, once I'd finished visiting all the places I absolutely wanted to see, I found that I still had one whole day left. My friend Govind, who had lived in Jodhpur since he was born, was helping me explore the city and had a surprise up his sleeve. He asked me to get onto his motorcycle and play Hot and Cold for the next 35 minutes till we reached somewhere that he refused to tell me more about.

Have you ever played Hot and Cold? It's a guessing game in which you try and identify a place or thing that someone has in mind by asking them questions or naming things. If what you have said is somewhat correct, the person replies, 'Hot!' If it has little or nothing to do with the object or place, they reply, 'Cold!' From my pillion seat, I started naming things and places, and Govind would tell me if my answer was hot or cold.

'Another fort?' I began.

He swung his head from side to side and gave me a muffled 'Cold!' from under his helmet.

'Ummm...a lake!' I tried again.

'*Very* cold!' he laughed.

'A museum?' I asked hopefully.

'Very hot,' he said encouragingly, and prodded me to guess what kind of museum he had in mind.

But no matter what I said, his answer was always 'Cold', 'Very cold' and once even 'Freezing!'. By this point, we had reached the outskirts of Jodhpur, and the narrow city roads had turned into trails flanked by dry grassy hills in the distance. Once we left the city, there were hardly any houses around, just a vast expanse of faded brown hills on both sides of the road. Once in a while we would come across a shepherd in a bright red turban and white kurta-dhoti, grazing his sheep. I wondered what kind of museum would be located amongst the hills. Just when I'd run out of guesses, we turned into a large gate. The sign outside read 'Arna Jharna – The Thar Desert Museum'.

Govind parked, and we got off and walked to the ticket counter. A moustached man was snoozing away in the heat of the June afternoon, his head resting on his palm. 'Rrrrrr,' he snored rhythmically. Govind had to nudge the man thrice to wake him up. Finally, he woke up and smiled apologetically. 'Not too many people come in the afternoon, you see,' he said and handed us our tickets.

The museum was *nothing* like I'd ever seen before. It was like entering a village in the middle of the sand dunes of Rajasthan. The museum was built in the style of local homes, complete with rust-coloured walls and thatched roofs. There were a number of small rooms scattered all over the complex, and each housed a different collection of things. Govind told me that the museum was conceived by one of India's most famous folklorists (storytellers) and oral historians, Mr Komal Kothari. In a career spanning more than 50 years, he'd made sure that many of the lesser-known artists and musicians of Rajasthan got to showcase their work to the world. He'd built the Arna Jharna Museum to show people the most important aspects of local life in Rajasthan and to use the space for music performances.

We walked through the different sections for an hour – folk instruments, pottery, puppets – until we finally came to the gallery that Govind really wanted to show me. We bent our heads to go through a small door and into a large hall that was covered with...*brooms*. Yes, brooms!

This simple household object was the most interesting part of our visit! In that small room, there were over 160 brooms from different parts of the state on display. Each exhibit had a description of how the broom had been made, the bush or tree that it got its body and stalks from, ways of making the broom and which communities use it.

Why brooms, you ask? Well, Govind told me that brooms in Rajasthan are made from different plants depending on where they were being made. For example, if you live in a place called Barmer, you're likely to have a *khemep* broom, made from a *khemep* shrub. This grows in abundance near Barmer, and people use its stalks to make their brooms. In the same way, there was a *siniya* (used in Jodhpur) broom, a *daab* (used in Jalore) broom and many others on display. Some were big, some were small, some were bushy, while some had very few stalks. But all of them were good for the purpose of sweeping and cleaning dusty rooms!

We must have spent an hour in this unique gallery, stopping by every broom and reading about its history.

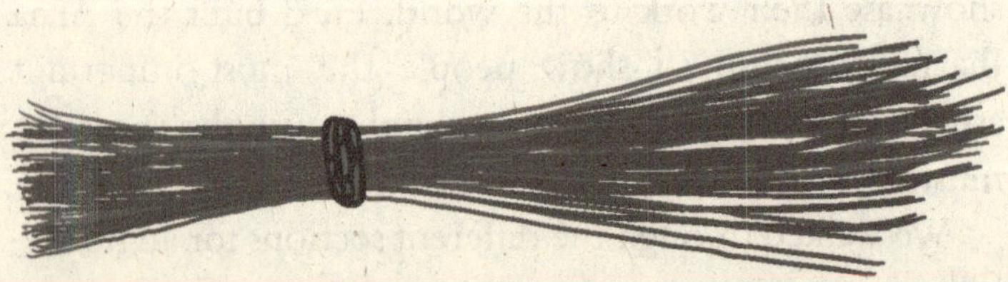

I thought of the broom in my home and realized how little I knew about it – nothing about its history, cool beginnings, or the style in which it was made!

I was suddenly very inspired. I went home, took out all the stalks of the lemongrass bush in my garden and tried tying them together. It looked good enough to me, but honestly, all the dust remained in the room once I was done cleaning. I guess should have paid attention to the sweeping part as well!

How to Get to Arna Jharna

You can get to Jodhpur by flight or train from anywhere in India. The Arna Jharna Museum is located about 20 kilometres northeast of the city in a village called Moklawas, and it takes about 30 minutes to get there by road.

The Joys of Jodhpur

Govind runs a company called Blue City Walks, which takes visitors to some very interesting locations across Jodhpur. You can join him or any other tour to do some of my favourite things in the city, like:

- Feeding the kites at the Mehrangarh Fort
- Hearing the Mehrangarh Fort band practise in the afternoons
- Meeting the goats at Amar Bakrashala (a sanctuary for goats saved from slaughter)
- Visiting the Ghanta Ghar – A four-storey clock tower that stands at the beginning of Sadar Bazar in the city and is home to a giant clock that needs to be wound manually

A Shrine for a Bike

Have you ever gone on a road trip on a highway? Well, if you have, you couldn't have missed the many places you can pray at along both sides of the rather broad roads all across the country. You may have seen temples weighed under bells and colourful sculptures, with never-ending queues of people outside. Or you would have seen simple shrines housed below trees, with only a smear of orange for an idol. You would have also spotted the white-washed walls of mosques and onion-shaped domes of gurdwaras. Places of worship are never hard to find when you're travelling around India, and I've seen my fair share of them. I mostly bow my head slightly to offer a small prayer while I'm zipping by, but I always make sure to stop at the *really* interesting ones. And amongst the shrines dedicated to dogs, clocks, rats and planes that I've seen across the length and breadth of the country, there's one that needed more than just a short stop. It was a temple that left me bewildered.

Can you imagine – the object of everyone's devotion was a motorcycle? I *swear* I rubbed my eyes twice to believe what I was seeing.

One winter, I was travelling around Rajasthan, and I had just left the city of Jodhpur to go south, towards a town called Pali. The taxi was trundling down the highway, and the driver and I were chatting about life in the desert state, when we spotted a huge commotion by the road in a village called Chotila. All the traffic seemed to be slowing down in front of one particular spot. I could see people in cars and on bikes bow their heads to the left and then speed up again. Closer to the spot where people were bowing their heads, there was a long queue of devotees snaking inwards from the highway. I asked my driver to park ahead along the road and decided to join this long line of people, who were inching forward slowly. I had to see this with my own eyes!

Finally, I reached a small platform, a couple of steps higher than where we were standing, which was bursting with people jostling to look at something I couldn't yet see. After pushing my way past a number of people, flowers and incense sticks in their hands, I finally managed to see the object of their love. It was a rusty black bike with marigold flowers arranged gingerly on its handles. It had a vermilion *tika* smeared on the headlight, and a faded photograph of a gentleman with a slim moustache was propped against a stand next to the bike. The devotees moved close to the bike and respectfully offered it a prayer, sweets and incense sticks.

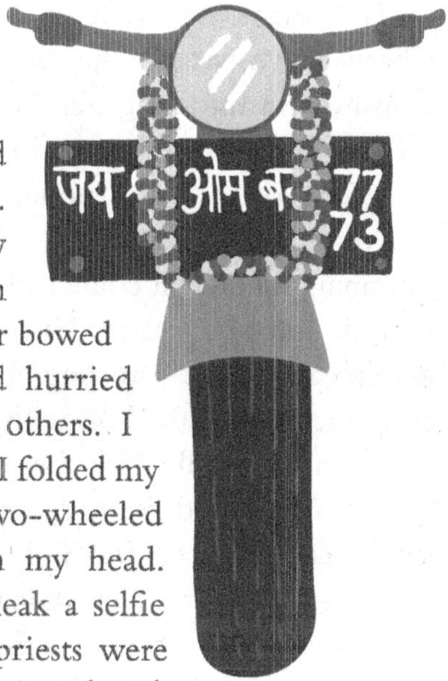

A sculpture of the same moustached man, more religious things and two priests occupied a part of the platform. The two priests quickly took the offerings from the people, touched their bowed heads, blessed them and hurried them to make way for others. I had nothing to offer, but I folded my hands in front of the two-wheeled 'idol' and got a pat on my head. Some people tried to sneak a selfie with the bike, but the priests were beginning to get rather irritated with anyone who slowed down the line. 'Chalo, chalo!' they said grouchily.

Squeezing myself out of the chaotic crowd, I stood in the shade of a small hut close by to soak in what was happening from a distance. The hut doubled up as a shop selling chips and bottles of water, and offered shade to those who wanted a break from the scorching sun. The owner, Ramesh, greeted me with a smile and asked if this was the first time I was visiting Om Banna's shrine. Looking at my confused expression, he told me the story of the shrine, stopping at just the right places to judge my expressions and reactions. (I gave him the satisfaction of feeling like a great storyteller by gasping and giggling at all the right times.)

The shrine was built to commemorate Om Banna, Chotila's own avatar of the almighty. Om was a young man who lived in the village, and he was known for his deep love for his glitzy black motorcycle. The Royal Enfield bike (one of the most popular motorcycles in India – you've probably seen it a thousand times) made a loud thumping sound that could be heard from a distance when he rode into the village. His neighbours would see him get up early in the morning, fetch a bucket of water and clean each part of the bike with great precision. Once spic and span, he would kick the bike to start it, the distinct 'thud, thud' sound filling the neighbourhood. He always left a wake of dust behind him. But sadly, Om Banna's love affair with his motorcycle didn't last too long.

In 1991, he met with a fatal accident while riding. He had been riding too fast one night, and he hit a tree by the side of the road, just before entering the village. Soon, the police arrived, investigated the accident spot and took the bike to the closest police station. They said that the bike had to be kept there until the investigation was over. However, the cops had no clue that something strange was in store for them! The very first night the bike disappeared. A team was sent to find the missing bike, and after searching for a while, they found it in the same spot where the accident had taken place.

'That's strange!' exclaimed the leader of the search party. They wheeled it back, trying to see if any of the local pranksters were responsible for this. The cops parked it at the police station again, dusted their hands and went back to snoozing through the night.

The next night, when the clock struck 12, *exactly* the same thing happened again! The bike was gone with no signs of someone having driven it off. Now the cops knew where they would find it, and it was promptly brought back. Each night, the bike would disappear and be found at the same spot of the accident.

This went on for more than two weeks. At first, the cops thought this was the work of a smart but annoying prankster, so they took out all the fuel from the bike's tank, but it STILL went missing every night!

It's then that the cops got a bit nervous. Some say that every night the bike would rumble to life by itself and then magically disappear. Fearful that Om Banna's spirit might have possessed the bike, it was moved from one station to another.

A few weeks after the accident, Om Banna's mother dreamt that this would only stop when a shrine was built precisely where the accident took place. By then, the cops were exhausted by the disappearing bike and didn't want to provoke the ghost (if there was one at all), so they immediately agreed.

The bike was brought to its current spot and placed on a platform. Almost magically, no further spooky activity was recorded!

Other Spooky Destinations in Rajasthan

Bhangarh: Bhangarh was established in 1573. In 1783, the town was hit by famine and the people either left or died here. Since then, no one has lived in this place. The temples, shops, mosques and a palace remain uninhabited.

Kuldhara Village: This prosperous village was abandoned in the nineteenth century. Some say it was because of an earthquake. Others believe it's the lack of water supply here. Whatever may be the case, no one has lived here in the last 200 years.

Jagatpura: This village is believed to be a haunt for witches.

Sudhabay: This small village organizes an annual fair for people possessed by evil spirits.

Rana Kumbha Palace: It is said that the palace is haunted by Maharani Padmini, who lived here centuries ago.

How to Reach Chotila

You need to take a flight or train to Jodhpur. The massive Mehrangarh Fort is the centre of attraction in this city. From here, you can take a taxi and go 50 kilometres south to the village of Chotila. You will be able to spot the shrine easily, as there are always large crowds outside it.

The Spectacular Stepwells of India

How would you feel if I told you that there's going to be no water in the taps in your home, no long showers allowed and no cold water or ice in the fridge starting right now? Sounds unimaginable, right? But this was *exactly* how people lived hundreds of years ago. There were no systems of pipes that transported water to homes and no geysers or showers for long, leisurely baths. Refrigerators for household use only came in about 100 years ago, so there were no ice cubes tinkling in glasses before then! Water had to be carried on foot from distant rivers, wells and lakes, stored in buckets and other containers, and then drinking water was cooled in earthen pots. It was a tough life!

People in some villages and towns were lucky, as they lived close to rivers or wells. But some regions in India, especially in states like Rajasthan, Gujarat and Madhya Pradesh, lay in the middle of dry, parched lands with little access to natural water. The rulers of these places were always worried for the people of their kingdom. To make things easier, some kings, especially in Gujarat, came up with the idea of building large tanks surrounded by steps on all sides. These would serve the purpose of storing water as well as add to the architectural splendour of their kingdoms. These structures were called *baoris*, or stepwells. I love the idea of stepwells and have seen many of them during my travels – let me introduce you to two of my favourite ones.

Panna Meena Baori, Jaipur

A curved, yellow-walled pathway snakes up to the ancient Amber Fort perched on a hilltop in Jaipur. Halfway through the walk up to the fort, if you leave the path and steer right into a narrow street, you will reach the *baori* of Panna Meena. This ancient waterbody lies hidden right under the noses of the swarms of visitors that throng Amber Fort, one of Jaipur's most popular tourist destinations. Meanwhile, it is *very* unlikely that you will see a busload of tourists clamouring

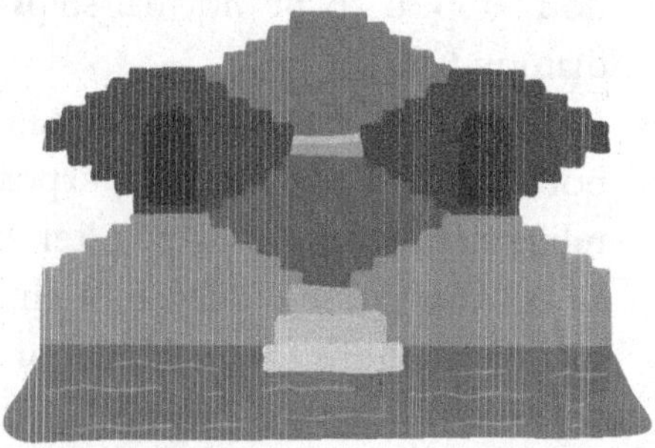

to see this stepwell. This grand, deep, eight-storeyed *baori* was constructed by Panna Meena, a minister in the court of Maharaja Ram Singh, a former king of Jaipur, who ruled the city from 1835 to 1880.

Hundreds of years ago, areas around the fort were reserved for the people of Amber city to build homes and businesses. Given the very dry landscape of the region, building a water storage system for daily use was important. Panna Meena constructed this stepwell as a symbol of his responsibility as a minister and to provide relief to those who lived nearby. Neat steps descend to a pool of murky green water, where fish and turtles get respite from the brutal heat. Zig-zagging steps surround this well, and a pathway runs all along the top for people to walk on. Four dome-shaped pavilions lie in each corner above the *baori*. These corners offer shade and a resting place for anyone who is tired from roaming around in the heat.

What I love best about this *baori* is the hundreds of steps going down to the water in a beautiful pattern. When you stand in one corner and look at them, they don't appear to be normal steps but form a spectacular diamond shape.

Like many *baori*s in Rajasthan, this tank was built for both practical and social purposes, and gatherings and religious ceremonies were often held around the well.

All you can see today, though, is a few locals using the shaded pavilions for an afternoon snooze.

Adalaj ni Vav, Ahmedabad, Gujarat

This breathtakingly beautiful thirteenth-century stepwell, known as a *vav* in Gujarati, lies about 15 kilometres from Ahmedabad. It was built by Mahmud Begada in 1411 to commemorate Queen Rudabai, the wife of Veersinh, a local chieftain. The people from the surrounding villages once filled water from this stepwell. It has wonderful intricate carvings on the pillars that support its five storeys, and its beams also function as pit stops for pigeons flying in to rest. This stepwell represents the Indo-Islamic style of architecture that can be seen in many stepwells of the same period.

I find a number of things really fascinating about this *vav*. For example, the opening in the ceiling above the landing allows both light and air to enter the octagonal well, but direct sunlight never touches the steps except at noon. It is said that the temperature inside the well is six degrees lower than the outside. The stepwell has three entrance stairways, which meet at the first-storey underground. When you look up from here, the opening in the sky is shaped like an octagon. The walls are covered in carvings of mythological creatures and everyday scenes from rural life. Some of the carvings include the Ami Khumbor (a pot that contains the water of life) and the Kalp Vriksha (the tree of life) carved out of a single slab of stone. There is a popular local belief that the small carving of the *navagraha* (nine planets) towards the edge of the well protects the monument from bad luck.

Getting to Jaipur and Ahmedabad

Both Jaipur and Ahmedabad are well connected by flights, trains and road to major Indian cities, as you know by now. Once you reach Ahmedabad, you can take a taxi to cover the 15-kilometre distance to the Adalaj ni Vav.

Other Beautiful Stepwells in the Country

- **Agrasen ki Baoli, Delhi:** This fourteenth-century stepwell was built by King Agrasen.
- **Chand Baori, Abhaneri:** Located 90 kilometres from Jaipur, this stepwell has 3,500 steps and 13 storeys. It was built by King Chanda of the Nikhumba dynasty.
- **Surya Kund, Modhera:** Located in Gujarat, this was built in 1026-27 BCE, during the reign of Bhima I of the Chaulukya dynasty.
- **Dada Harir Stepwell, Ahmedabad:** Built in the fifteenth century, this stepwell has excellent carvings on the walls.
- **Shahi Baoli, Lucknow:** This *baoli* has five storeys and was built by the Mughals.

When the Gods Grant Visas

Just like many other temples in India, the Chilkur Balaji Temple in Hyderabad has a chaotic and busy entrance. The road leading up to the structure has stalls selling heaps of flowers of every imaginable colour, incense sticks and puja ingredients. You'll also find men calling out, offering to keep your shoes safely while you go into the shrine. At the end of the road, you can see a tall blue building with a gopuram that has lots of mythical creatures carved into it – that's the main temple. But before you can get there, you need to wade through a sea of people and a constant stream of noise and chatter.

I was inching closer to the shrine, behind a huge rush of people, when someone shook a piece of white paper in front of my legs. I looked to my left, and from behind a heap of yellow flowers peeped out a lady with a toothy smile, who waved at me to stop. She was sitting on the road beside her flower basket, and I bent down so that she could hand me the crisp white paper and a pen. The paper had a grid of 108 boxes printed on it. I looked at it in confusion. What on earth was I supposed to do with this?

'Go, go,' she said. 'You'll need it – 108 rounds and a visa!' In a hurry to get into the premises and confident that I would learn what to do with this paper and pen from other people, I went ahead, one tiny step at a time.

Now I didn't actually need a visa to anywhere, but I was curious to see this temple and learn about its funny connection with visas. I was writing about cool temples in India, and this had great potential to make it to the list.

In Hyderabad, the Chilkur Balaji Temple, popularly known as the Visa Balaji Temple, is famous as the shrine that grants its devotees visas to visit the USA. (When you travel to another country, along with a ticket, you need a visa that allows you to go to that country for a certain period of time.)

A lot of the young working people in the city are 'techies', who work with apps, computers, websites and all that stuff. And there are lots of great tech companies in the USA, where they aspire to work. Perhaps these people have their reasons to trust that Lord Balaji will put in a good word with the visa officials! The temple first became famous in the 1980s, when many people praying here started obtaining visas to the USA very easily. Can you imagine the rush in this temple after this news became common knowledge? It is said that between seventy-five thousand and one lakh devotees visit the shrine each week, especially on Fridays and Sundays, which are considered auspicious. My advice would be to go on any other day because there'll be slightly less of a crowd.

I had gone on a Saturday, but it took 30 minutes of tiny steps forward in the queue to reach the main door of the temple. Once I entered the complex, I saw a courtyard with a shrine in the middle. The crowd in front of me split into four queues, and from there everyone began to walk around the shrine in a clockwise circle. By then, I had noticed that all the people around me were also clutching a white piece of paper and a pen.

After completing one circle, I noticed the person in front of me ticking one box on the grid. When a second round was completed, he ticked off another box. Ah, now I'd got it! The grid was to be used to keep count of how many circles one had finished. I ticked my first and second boxes too and continued to be swept along with the crowd. Phew, it was tiring work. I must have done about 20 rounds when I decided that I'd had quite enough of all the rotation. I didn't even need a visa!

I quietly slunk out of the line and watched from a corner as hundreds of people continued to make their way around the shrine. *The US visa officials must come and see this someday*, I thought to myself. *If not for anything else, they should give these devotees their visas just for all the effort!*

Other Religious Hotspots for Visas

- **Shaheed Baba Nihal Singh Gurdwara**: Located in the Talhan village of Punjab, close to Ludhiana, the 150-year-old Shaheed Baba Nihal Singh Gurdwara is also known as the Visa Gurdwara. You can see the building from a distance, as it has a huge model of an airplane perched on top. Devotees form long queues to place small model airplanes in front of the main shrine. You can see rows of planes arranged before the Guru Granth Sahib, the holy book of the Sikhs.
- **Khadia Hanuman Temple**: A popular mythological story talks about Hanuman, the monkey god, flying over cities and hills to carry a mountain to Ram. His flying skills might be the reason why people think Hanuman can help get them a visa. It's no wonder the Khadia Hanuman Temple in Ahmedabad is known for its visa-procuring powers.
- **Bajrangbali Temple**: Even though there are hundreds of Hanuman temples in New Delhi, the one on IGNOU Road in South Delhi is known amongst devotees to help make their visa wishes come true. People write thank-you notes in the temple register after they have received their visas.

Wonderful Walks

Trekking in Tadiandamol

Do you know what the word 'sentry' means? It means a soldier who keeps guard over a place or controls who can go in. That's always seemed like a fairly big responsibility to me, and suddenly there I was, being a sentry in a group of four trekkers going camping in Karnataka.

Earlier that evening, our trek leader, Siddharth, had said that all four of us would not be able to sleep at the same time. Two people would be sentries for the campsite at one point, keeping watch for two hours, and then the other two would take their place. We would have to take turns all night till the sun came out and it was time to trek up.

We were at the base of the Tadiandamol Peak in Coorg, the third-highest mountain in Karnataka. It was just 7 p.m., but night had already arrived with a full moon suspended in the sky and the stars scattered around. How brightly they shone because of the clear skies and lack of pollution. You'd have no such luck in the city.

But wait. Let me take you to the start of this story. I'm part of a trekking group that regularly organizes hikes that can be done without guides. These are usually relatively easy hikes with clear trails and are easily accessible from most cities. A few of us had chosen Tadiandamol, only six hours from Bengaluru, to climb over a weekend. Tadiandamol lies in Coorg, which is one of the biggest coffee producing regions in India. We had received all the details from the hiking group, and then we'd taken a bus and been dropped off at the base of the peak at 4 p.m. We would spend the night there and start walking up the next morning.

On the way there, we could see hillsides carpeted with coffee bushes. It was a beautiful landscape, and we couldn't wait to see the view from the top. We reached the base of Tadiandamol early enough to find a clearing and decided to pitch our tents before it got too dark. We were carrying strong torches and a battery-operated light, but we still gathered dry wood and twigs to make a bonfire. After eating some packaged food for dinner and chatting around the bonfire, we started yawning at about 8 p.m. That *never* happens to me in the city. When we were yawning more than we were talking, Sid mentioned sentry duty. He and I would have to go first, and then wake the other two after two hours, around 10 p.m.

Oh no! How would I *ever* keep my eyes open? But I had to – after all, it might just be a matter of life and death! You see, the reason we needed to be on sentry duty was that we were now close to a forest and needed to stay safe from wild animals. All regular trekkers know that wild animals usually stay away from groups of people, especially if they are talking and making noise. Our other two friends quickly huddled in their tent and soon, I could hear them snoring away. What a racket it was! Their snores sounded like bears having a conversation – I was pretty sure that any wild animal would be too scared to come near us.

Sid and I chatted through yawns, and even tried singing songs to keep awake. Being a sentry is no easy business. You have to be alert, keep a look-out for odd sounds and be brave enough to face any intrusion. And when your eyelids are heavy with sleep, two hours feels like two hundred hours. In fact, at one point, I nodded off and Sid had to shake me awake. Finally, the two hours were done and as soon as we hit the 120th minute, I went rushing into the tent and woke up the folks in line. The night was hardly peaceful, what with the broken sleep…and don't say it – I know I made a *lousy* sentry.

The next morning, our hike started out with a simple stroll through a coffee plantation, which opened up into a pale golden grassy meadow. Along the plantation, our necks were swinging this way and that to spot bee-eaters, velvet-fronted nuthatches, barbets and robins sitting in the thick coffee bushes and tall trees. Where the plantation ended, a mountain trail began in the meadow. At first, it was quite easy but soon, the strain of the incline uphill started telling on our thighs. As we went up the

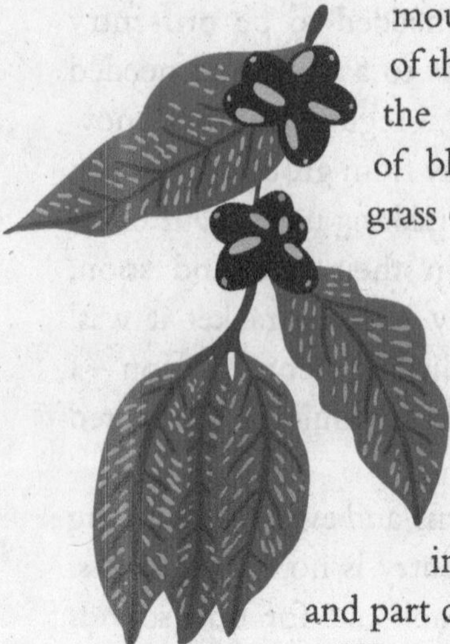

mountain, we had gorgeous views of the lower hills stacked one behind the other in every possible shade of blue. The yellow, sun-bleached grass on the hills also had some forest patches in the middle. These are called the Shola forests. These forest patches were filled with moss, tree roots, a dirt path and slim clear streams that we had to hop across. It was an interesting hike – part grassy hills and part deep forests.

We must have walked for about two hours, keeping our eyes peeled for birds and insects, when a rocky clearing ending in a cliff appeared. We had now reached the top of the peak, and we moved quickly towards the edge of the cliff, where a panoramic view of the valley, covered in a million shades of green, unfolded. Our group of four inched towards the edge to hang our legs over the side. After spending about half an hour at the cliff, we turned back before the blazing heat made it difficult to walk back.

Walking back was much easier than climbing uphill, and even though the climb was not that difficult, the day was exhausting in a good way. We reached the base by lunch and took a bus to a hotel where we were going to spend the night. Thankfully, this time no one had to be on sentry duty!

How to Get to the Basecamp

Tadiandamol lies in the south-east of Coorg and is most easily approached from a place called Kakkabe. From here, head one kilometre to Kaikamba village, from where a tar road leads up to the Nalknad Palace, an old palace where no one lives at the moment. You can start the trek from here or choose to go by a jeep which can drop you right till the end of the tar road (three kilometres). From this point, Tadiandamol is five kilometres away.

The Nalknad Palace

This crumbling two-storey structure is a key landmark on this trek. Take some time to saunter inside and see the old paintings that have been restored by the state archaeology department. The wooden-floored palace still has red pillars, a wedding *mantapa* (canopy created for a wedding ceremony to take place), the queen's quarters and beautiful paintings on the ceilings and walls intact. It was built in 1792 by King Dodda Veerarajendra as a hideaway from invading armies.

A Day at Tiger Falls

Before I say a word more, I want to make one thing clear – there are no tigers in or around this waterfall. Don't expect to find a yellow-and-black-striped big cat scrubbing itself under a cascade of water, cleaning its paws, loosening dirt from its teeth and swishing its tail. But you *will* definitely hear a loud ROAR! As you walk into the clearing, all you can hear is the booming sound of water thundering down a 50-metre-high rockscape. And it's *loud*!

Ol'... glub... Donald,
Had... glub... farm,
Eee... glub... eee... glub... wooooaaahh!

No, I haven't lost my mind. And no, I'm *not* singing the wrong song. This is just how my friends and I must have sounded singing 'Old MacDonald Had a Farm' under the rushing water of Tiger Falls. We'd already been singing the song for hours – it had been our anthem throughout the five-kilometre trek that started in a place called Viraatkhai and took us through some lovely meadows and villages, till we reached the frothy white sheet of water slung from the tall, high rock. The impact of the water was so great that it had created a small pool under the waterfall, and the cool water after a hard trek was so inviting that four people from our group of eight jumped right in. The rest of us took our time, gingerly testing the cool water with our feet, swallowing a big gulp of air and finally getting in.

Viraatkhai is a small village that lies in the lower part of the massive Himalayan mountains in the state of Uttarakhand. It is only 73 kilometres from Dehradun and takes about three hours to reach, even if you stop ten times to take photographs or admire the mountains from the viewpoints. Located 6,100 feet above sea level, it's usually cold here through the year, with sheets of fluffy clouds blanketing the village in the mornings and evenings. Viraatkhai has stunning views of craggy mountaintops and deep valleys that look like they will throw back endless echoes if you shout hard enough into them. I didn't try it, but you must if you go there!

It was January, and the sun had sunk behind the mountains as early as 5 p.m. The sky had turned an inky blue and then black in a matter of minutes, and the stars sparkled more brightly than the city lights. In the mountains, there's not much you can do in the dark, so we all scattered about the campsite to find dropped dry wood for a bonfire. It took us an hour to find a decent-sized heap that would keep the fire burning for two hours. Because of all the hard work we put into finding the wood, the fire felt much warmer and brighter than normal. It crackled once in a while, sending out a sudden sprinkle of golden embers. We sang songs and told many scary ghost stories, armed with a steady supply of food and drink. Finally, after the last plate of fries was devoured, all of us returned to our cosy rooms and got under our soft, lumpy quilts for the night.

The next day at 6 a.m., we woke up to a magical view of the valley in front of our cottages. The sky was filled to the brim with clouds. Only when the sunlight made its way over the mountains did the clouds disappear. By 8 a.m., it was the perfect weather for a short trek to Tiger Falls, which didn't seem too far. But you must remember, walking five kilometres in the hills is not easy. I realized that it wasn't stamina that we needed – it was willpower! Trailing behind a local guide, our platoon of young and old trekkers made easy progress initially. And then came the huffs and the puffs. Not a single one from the kids, though! They marched on easily, arm in arm with each other.

We were walking on a grassy hill with soft curves – not too steep but not that easy to climb either. Fresh green grass and delicate white and purple flowers covered the dips and the peaks of the hill. It looked like the grass and the flowers were battling to see who would cover the hill faster! While the ground we walked on looked like a painting, the sky was no less artistic – it was bright blue and streaked with fluffy white clouds. We also came across a few houses along the way, clinging on to the sides of the hills. The houses had very low roofs made of flat stones. (The low roofs help keep houses warm during winter, when it gets extremely cold.) What a lovely view of these green hills their bedrooms would have!

The sight of goats and mules feeding on the fresh green grass of the hills got our group singing 'Old MacDonald Had a Farm' continuously. All I could manage was an out-of-breath 'Ee ya ee ya o!' once in a while. Finally, after two hours, a hillside down, a hillside up and then down yet again, we reached the base of Tiger Falls.

What a magical sight it was! A bubbly veil of water covered a large rock behind it. We jumped right in and let the gushing water massage our sore backs. After an hour of playing about in the water, we draped ourselves across the boulders around the pool. It was finally time to dive into our picnic basket! The apples, sandwiches, cartons of juice and cookies felt good after our trek. I was ready to go to sleep there, the cool water at my feet, but something interesting was happening in one of the shallow ends of the pool of water.

Some of the younger people in my group were wading through the water, trapping tadpoles in plastic bottles and releasing them after some time. This game went on till it was time to head back. Even though tadpoles had replaced farm animals as the group's object of interest, the anthem for the trek was still 'Old MacDonald Had a Farm'. We sang it all the way back as well!

Trek to Tiger Falls

You can get to Dehradun by flight, train or bus and then go by road up to Viraatkhai. This trip is best done over three–four days.

Venture out around Viraatkhai

Here's a bunch of other fun things you can do around the village.

- **Deoban**: This is a forested area filled with deodar trees and offers panoramic views of the Himalayan ranges. It's home to a variety of birds, like Himalayan woodpeckers, white-collared blackbirds, green-backed tits and more.
- **Budher Caves**: Also known as Miola Caves, these are named after the German explorer who discovered them.
- **Mundali**: This is a skiing destination covered in powdery snow in the winter.

Jamun's Lunch Spot

There are very few things in the world that make me jealous. Right now, I can only think of Elsa the Snow Queen from the movie *Frozen* and a friend of mine who has three dogs. I love the way Elsa can turn anything into ice with just a swoosh of her finger, and her long locks do look pretty. But then she's just a character in a movie, so all my jealousy is actually just focused on my friend Divya.

A few years ago, Divya adopted three indie dogs, Tigress, Pari and Marco Polo, and they spend all their time travelling around the country by train. (Dogs are allowed only in first-class compartments of trains in India.) When I see photographs of her and her troop in ancient forts and green fields or beautiful hotels, I can't help but think, *I wish that were me.* Come to think of it, *her* life seems as fairy-tale-like as Elsa's. Hmpf.

But recently, I met a young boy who turned my skin into the shade of grass (not literally – don't worry!

I didn't become the Wicked Witch of the West). I was more jealous of him than Divya and her gang of furry buddies. Funnily, I met him while walking up a grassy hill, a million shades of green all around me.

I was visiting a small village called Kund in Uttarakhand. My friend Nandini, who has visited this region many times, knew that I was not too far from Deoriatal, a beautiful lake on top of a hill. The base of the trek is a village called Sari, which lies only 18 kilometres from Kund. So, on one of the days, I got up really early and asked for a drop to Sari village. Nandini had prepped me well. The hike up to Deoriatal would only take two hours, and since it wasn't that steep, I wouldn't even need a guide. But she kept the grand finale a surprise and asked me not to check any pictures of Deoriatal online. I kept my promise.

Sari village (which, by the way, has nothing to do with long, flowing pretty saris) had a few homes and shops. Someone at a shop was kind enough to point me in the direction of the trail. And so I started my climb. The muddy trail wended up the hill, ascending only very slightly with each bend, so it didn't feel like I was climbing up. Everything was still and quiet, except for the odd squeak or birdcall. Some parts of the hill were covered by tall, ancient-looking trees. The rest of it was blanketed in bright green. I was humming a tune, hoping to add to the melody of the birds, but we were certainly not in sync.

Suddenly I heard a sharp whistle. A bird? No, it couldn't be. The sounds of the birds here were coming from the top of trees, so they were slightly muffled. This was too clear. It was as if the bird was right behind me! *Feeee* – came the sound again. Sharp. Loud. Disturbing. I looked back and saw a young boy walking about 50 metres behind me. I waved at him and waited till he caught up with me.

'Did I scare you? I'm sure I did,' he said, grinning. I played along and nodded seriously.

The boy's name was Jamun, and he was ten years old. 'My mother had a *jamun* tree that she loved very much,' he explained. 'So she called me Jamun at home, then my friends started calling me that too, and now the whole Sari village knows me as Jamun.'

Suddenly I noticed that he wasn't alone. There were 20 sheep with him, occasionally straying off to nibble on the juicy grass all around. From a distance, they looked like white fluffy dots on the green hill. Jamun was a shepherd!

'Don't you go to school?' I asked.

'Oh, I go to the afternoon school,' he replied, and then launched into his routine. 'See, I wake up at five every day. Our home is on the edge of that hill,' he pointed in a direction, 'it's the one with the vegetable fields. There's no hill or house in front of our home for a long distance, so I get a clear view of the sunrise. Even though I've been seeing it every day for so many years, I still find it dazzling. Then after a quick breakfast and a hot cup of tea, I go to the shed to meet the sheep. They are impatient by the time I get there, crowding around the door to be let out. They know the drill pretty well. All of them follow me along the side of the road till we reach the base of the hike. You should see how excited they are when they get to the trail! Because after they are off the road, I just let them do whatever they want. We walk up slowly to the top of the hill to see the beautiful...'

'Wait, wait, wait. Stop. Please don't describe the lake just yet! I want it to be a surprise,' I interrupted just in time. Phew!

Jamun smiled and continued telling me about his day – about how he snoozed for some time at 11, when the sheep were full-bellied, and how they all took different spots under trees for their naps. Then they would start again in 45 minutes till they reached the peak. The sheep would drink water from the lake and eat some more green grass (they really do have quite an appetite!), and Jamun would eat his packed lunch. Even though the top of the mountain (at 8,000 feet) was a bit cooler than the village, it was bright and sunny on most days. He loved the fresh, crisp cool air on the top of the mountain. When everyone was well rested and bellies were full (again), all 21 of them would come trotting back home, Jamun leading the way and calling out to the stray sheep to stay with the group. Then, later in the day, he'd go to school for a few hours.

Well, that sounded like a great day to me! Waking up in the mountains to birdsong and not a horrible screechy alarm, go traipsing around the hills, nap under trees and eat picnic lunches and then go to school only for a few hours? I was a little jealous of him already!

Jamun and I had been talking for so long that I didn't realize that we had already reached the top. The path that we had taken had been flanked by thick foliage, and now suddenly there was a wide clearing. As we got closer, it was as if a curtain had got pulled off, and the picture that was revealed was out of this world!

In the middle of the bright green meadow was the shining Lake Deoriatal – which reflected the snowcapped peak of Mount Chaukhamba and the adjoining peaks! I'd never seen anything like it before!

Jamun looked at me and said cheekily, 'There, *that's* my lunch spot.'

How to Get to Deoriatal

Deoriatal is best accessed from Haridwar, which is the closest and most well-connected railway station. From here, Sari village is about 213 kilometres. The hike from here to Deoriatal is only three kilometres.

The Legend of Deoriatal

Deoriatal features in one of the stories in the Mahabharata. One day, when the Pandavas were exiled in the forest, the eldest brother, Yudhishthir, asked the other four (Arjun, Bhim, Nakul and Sahadev) to look for water. The youngest brother found this lake and was about to take a sip of the water when a demon appeared and asked him a question. When Sahadev could not answer the question, he died on the spot. The same happened to the three other brothers when each of them went in search of the ones who had disappeared and, overcome by thirst, tried to take a sip of the lake's water. Finally, it was Yudhishthir's turn. The demon appeared again, and asked him, 'If I had to bring any of your brothers back to life, whom would you want it to be?' Yudhishthir was a kind, compassionate and fair man. He said, 'My brother Nakula, as it would be an injustice to my stepmother, Madri, if I asked for Bhim or Arjun. For she would lose both her sons, unlike my mother Kunti, who would at least have me.' The demon, who was really the god Yama in disguise, was happy with the answer and brought back all four to life again.

A Bridge of Roots

One of the good things about travelling a lot is that very few things scare you, because you've had so many different experiences. Mountains that touch the sky and buildings as high? Those are just fine. White-water rafting and eating ants? That's okay too! But if I have to cross a bridge (doesn't matter if it's strong or dangly) with a frothy river flowing under it? My legs turn to jelly, I break into a cold sweat and start feeling extremely nervous. It doesn't matter how strong the bridge is, and that trucks and buses are zipping across it, I simply have shaky legs.

The last time this happened was in a small, green village called Nongriat in the state of Meghalaya. The bridge in question was not made of sturdy things like cement, stones or metal, but the *roots of trees*. Yes, yes, you heard right. Roots. Like the things that keep trees in the ground? Those roots. Now, for someone who's scared of bridges, this was terrifying. Luckily, the river below was calm and still.

But let me tell you how I got there in the first place.

Have you heard of a town called Cherrapunji in Meghalaya? Well, it's always been on my list of places to visit, because I'd heard that it's perpetually covered in cottony clouds and surrounded by intensely green hills. It used to be the wettest place on earth for a long time, because it got the highest amount of rainfall, but then it got upstaged by another town close by called Mawsynram.

After what seemed like many years of planning, I finally reached Cherrapunji in the summer of 2017. The weather was perfect for the hills – bright and sunny, and a cool breeze blew all through the day. I booked myself into a hotel in Cherrapunji for three nights and went about the small town to see the various popular locations. There are waterfalls around every corner in Cherrapunji – I think I counted at least a million! There are also caves that one can trek to, and various viewpoints from the top of hills, from where one can gaze at cloud-filled valleys. (The clouds here settle into the V-shape of the valleys like they're being poured into a cup!)

On the second day, the hotel owner, a man called Rimen, asked me how my day was going and if I had trekked to Nongriat village yet. 'It's very famous for its root bridges – you just can't miss it,' he exclaimed. Knowing that locals usually have the best suggestions for places to see, I wrote down the directions to Nongriat, thinking that there was no harm in seeing this root bridge from a *safe* distance. That wouldn't be so bad now, would it?

So, the next day, I booked myself a cab early in the morning and reached a village called Tyrna, from where I had to walk to Nongriat. But soon, I realized that reaching Nongriat was no easy feat at all! I had to go down a hill from Tyrna, walking down 2,500 tiny stone steps into the valley, and then climb up a few hundred more to finally get to the village.

Luckily, I met a guide called Ebinesan, who was standing at the start of the steps. While I was still deciding if I should actually go on this 2,500-step journey, his warm smile and walking tips helped me decide to go ahead. 'You can't miss it,' he said, sounding just like Remin. He even agreed to come with me, even though he had just come up the steps.

Wow! Ebinesan must be REALLY enthusiastic about showing people the root bridges, I thought to myself.

At first, walking down the steps seemed easy. They wound their way down a path that was flanked by trees bearing oranges, pomelos, guavas, jackfruits, areca, bay leaves and other woodland treasures. The smell of the fruits and spices was energizing. It took us a good two hours to get to the base of the hill and then another half an hour to reach Nongriat. The tiny village barely had any homes. Some other travellers had walked down as well, and were resting, massaging their legs, at a shop selling snacks and water bottles. It had certainly been a long walk, and a massage *did* feel good. I flopped on the ground too, kneading my calves with my hands. Ebinesan was impatient though; he wanted me to hurry up and see what we had come to set our eyes on.

It was about 11 a.m. by now. A few more minutes of walking and we came to a gentle creek with the water glistening in the sunlight. It was surrounded by loads of shrubs and tall trees with creepers clinging onto them for dear life. And across it was the most beautiful bridge I had ever seen. It was made entirely out of roots. Long, sturdy roots were curved around each other like big fat snakes, and they stretched from one end of the stream to the other. It was wide enough for two people to walk along. AND it was a double-decker bridge – which means it had two paths, one on top of each other, so that many people could walk on it at the same time! We sat at the edge of the stream so I could see this fabulous bridge properly. Ebinesan finally sat down beside me and told me the story behind these bridges.

These bridges are very popular in this part of Meghalaya, and they are made by the elders of the villages using a traditional, time-tested method. The young roots of the Ficus elastica trees (rubber trees) are placed inside long, hollow bamboo branches so they can straighten and stretch. Then, the elders patiently tie these roots together to make sure they are strong enough to walk on. Since the roots grow slowly inside the bamboo branches, it takes a very long time for the bridge to be completed, usually between 25 to 40 years. This means that the person who starts building this bridge is only thinking of the next generation, as they may not even be able to use it in their own lifetime. 'There are plenty of these bridges in Cherrapunji and the neighbouring areas, but few are as famous as this one. C'mon, we should get across!' said Ebinesan. I froze.

But Ebinesan would not listen to me or my fears. He pulled me onto the start of the bridge and promised me that it was really strong and that there was no way I would fall off. Besides, the river below was only two-feet deep – nothing bad would happen!

Taking a deep breath, I pressed my eyes closed, held onto Ebinesan's hands, who was facing me and walking backwards. He kept talking to me constantly: 'Good, good! Very good. Walk slowly.' Suddenly, he asked me to open my eyes saying that we had reached the end. The moment I opened them, I realized that I was bang in the middle of the bridge! My heart started thumping loudly in my chest and the familiar jelly feeling gripped my legs. 'Aaaaaaaaa,' my scream echoed in the otherwise quiet hills of Nongriat. No matter how pretty the bridge was, or how strong the roots were, I was still the same old Ms Jelly Legs!

Other Things to See in Cherrapunji

- **Nohkalikai Waterfall:** This is the tallest plunge waterfall (a waterfall that drops vertically without touching any rocks while falling) in India (340 metres).
- **Dainthelen Waterfall:** The special thing about this fall is that you can walk up to the head of the waterbody. When the water level is low in the summer, you can see the rockscape from where it falls quite clearly. It looks like hundreds of potholes!
- **Mawsmai Caves:** Go to this network of caves to see the natural formations inside.
- **Thangkharang Park:** If you want to stroll through gardens with rare plants and look at Bangladesh in the distance, this is where you want to go!
- **Nohsngithiang Waterfall** (yes, another one!): This is a group of seven waterfalls that falls from a U-shaped rockscape.

How to Get to Cherrapunji

This gorgeous place lies 150 kilometres away from the closest airport, which is in Guwahati, Assam. From here, you can take a taxi and reach Tyrna, and then you know, it's just another 2,500 steps and some more!

A Mountain Adventure

If you ever find yourself travelling in the lower regions of the Himalayas, keep your eyes peeled for white specks on the steep mountainsides that surround you. These specks are mountain goats! You'll see hordes of them nibbling away on the juicy grass all around them. They keep their heads close to the ground, looking up only to see if someone is approaching. They have no fear of heights and have so much strength that they can bound up the highest parts of a mountain – sometimes thousands of feet high – with ease. I wish I could do that! Now I'm no mountain goat, but I did try and climb to a height of over 13,000 feet once!

The Chopta-Tungnath-Chandrashila trek in the Uttarakhand Himalayas is actually a pretty easy hike – if you're a mountain goat. For me, it was a lung-bursting effort of over five whole hours, but one that had some pretty sweet rewards at the end. Before I tell you what they were, let me go back to the beginning.

It was a warm April day in Chopta, a small village in the heart of Uttarakhand. This region lies at the base of the mighty Himalayan mountains. It was the kind of day where it's hard to decide whether you should wear your fleece jacket or not. A leafy, shaded area would make your teeth chatter, but the moment you stepped into the sun, it was too hot to be comfortable in a T-shirt and shorts. I was working on a project close to Chopta and decided to reward myself by going on a short hike around the region.

Seeing my enthusiasm for the outdoors, the cook at the hotel I was staying at suggested that I try the Tungnath-Chandrashila trek. The trek starts from the Chopta village and takes you through beautiful meadows with a slight incline up till Tungnath Temple. Then comes the steep climb to the peak of the hill, called Chandrashila, from where you get a clear view of snow-topped Himalayan peaks as far as your eyes can see. 'It will be no trouble for you,' he said, making me feel quite confident.

My driver, Vikramji, took me to the base of the hill, and the rest was up to me. I thought it would be nice to have some company and tried to convince Vikramji to stretch his legs and hike up with me.

Despite my many attempts to convince him, his mind was made up. 'Look at this tummy,' he said, patting his big, round belly that always walked before him. 'There's no way I'm hauling myself and this sack to the top of the mountain. You go on. I'll wait right here – I promise!'

How hard could it be, I asked myself. From the bottom of the hill, the long trail ahead looked easy. *Just keep steady and keep walking. Get a rhythm going in your footsteps and the four kilometres to Tungnath should be easy-peasy*, I told myself. I wasn't sure if I could manage climbing the extra kilometre to reach Chandrashila, the highest point on this route. I looped the arms of my jacket tightly around my waist and started on the steep but steady trail. The bright sun kept my knee joints well oiled, and the rolling green meadows provided a stunning view and cheerful company. Yep, you guessed it! The green mountain was the perfect lunching spot for scores of mountain goats. The air was cool despite the sun, and the pine, deodar and rhododendron trees looked like they were touching the blue sky.

But it wasn't just me and the goats on the route. Long lines of tired-looking ponies weighed down by burly tourists and their luggage trotted ahead of and behind me. The jingle of their bells echoed in the valley and worked exactly like a horn, making sure everyone in the path stepped aside as they made their way to the Tungnath Temple.

There was also another creature that had sneaked in at my heels – a big black hairy *bhutiya* dog, who could easily go by the name Bhaloo. Bhaloo seemed to be from the Chopta village because he was well versed with the trail. He came up confidently next to me and I forged a friendship with him with a few pats.

The newly christened Bhaloo thus appointed himself my companion and walked close to me, as if we were

old trekking buddies. If he happened to speed up a little every now and then, he would quickly remind himself that he had company and pause till I caught up with him. He would often stop to lick the cool, melted ice water trickling down the hillside and then come right back to my side with a few bouncy steps. He'd clearly done this trek hundreds of times. 'Good boy!' I thanked Bhaloo and stroked his thick, mane-like fur.

About an hour into the walk, I spotted a small shanty with colourful biscuits, chips and packets of Maggi draped over every side. It was the perfect spot to take a short break, and Bhaloo also stopped and hopped on a chair, curling up for a quick snooze. I wolfed down my Maggi and started trundling up the mountain again with Bhaloo. Soon, I could see the top of the Tungnath Temple calling to me like a beacon. Even though it looked like it wasn't that far away, there was at least another hour of climbing left to do. *Phew! How do the mountain goats do it?*

After climbing for two hours, Bhaloo doggedly still at my heels, I could see a flutter of activity involving some priests and devotees. The Tungnath Temple is said to be over one thousand years old, and it even finds a place in Hindu mythology because it is associated with the Pandavas from the Mahabharata. My trusted doggy friend and I stopped for a quick peek and found a sturdy rock at the edge of the hill, from which we could admire the mountains on all sides. Rows of neat Vs lay between the stacks of mountains. Small clusters of villages added a dash of colour to the gorgeous green landscape. In the distance, the verdant hills were replaced by towering white mountains.

With no one else to share this experience with, Bhaloo, the poor, poor dog, was subjected to my constant commentary of how stunning the view was. By this point, I was tired and felt like I had walked high enough. I was just getting ready to turn back when a lean saffron-robed man, possibly a monk, zipped by me, turning only to gesture to me to follow him. I was confused at first. Did he mean me or someone else? But there was no one else around, so it had to be me. Despite being tired, I was curious and decided to follow him.

Wow, he was fast! I wondered if he spent his time hanging out with mountain goats.

I leapt up, dusted off my hands and followed in the man's footsteps. *Why did he gesture to me? Does he know me? Why is he alone?* Thankfully, Bhaloo followed too, and we were off on the last one kilometre up to the Chandrashila peak. This *really* tested my trekking prowess. With no particular trail to follow, we trudged up the hill using the tracks created by this lean leader of our pack of three. The area was covered in a dusting of day-old snow, glistening like diamonds under the bright sunlight. The sprightly sage dashed well ahead but looked back to see if I hadn't toppled over, feet up, head down on the track.

He didn't say a word, but he smiled encouragingly once in a while.

I'm pretty sure Bhaloo was questioning the wisdom of following me. He was clearly concentrating on not slipping. No clanking of pony bells followed on this route. No one hollered a namaste from the shanties. It was eerily quiet, and it took us an hour and more to finally emerge at the top of this mountain at 13,100 feet. Here, an ethereal landscape was waiting for us. Famous Himalayan peaks like Bandarpoonch, Kedar and Chaukhamba stood before us, covered in gleaming, pristine white. It was a 360-degree view of snowy splendour, and I was left speechless!

Spellbound by the scenery for over half an hour, I almost forgot that I had the sage for company. He had propped himself up at the edge of the mountain, sitting straight-backed. I walked up to him but chose to leave him undisturbed, as his eyes were closed. But I just couldn't understand why he would miss such a fantastic view. When about an hour had passed and the sky was just beginning to turn pink, I decided to thank him for encouraging me to come to this spot. Also, I had lots of questions. Why was he alone? Did he live here? Where did he come from? When was he planning to go back?

I cleared my throat twice to catch his attention. Finally, he looked at me and smiled. There! Now I would have the answers to all my questions. But the sage put his finger to his lips and closed his eyes calmly, indicating that he had taken a vow of silence. Leaving him to meditate in peace, I whistled to my other friend so that we could start walking back, but he had found himself a spot right next to the sage. He'd found companionship in a non-speaking partner as well.

Walking down was much faster and easier, and by now I was quite sure of my steps in the hills. I did miss Bhaloo, though. Vikramji welcomed me with a big smile when I got back to the car, and asked me all about the solo hike. What was my favourite part? Did I find it beautiful?

It was, no doubt, one of the best mountain vistas I had ever seen, but I had to think long and hard about the 'favourite' part. It was a tussle between the snow-capped peaks, Bhaloo's company and meeting the mysterious sage!

How Do You Climb This Mountain?

Sign up with a tour company like the Great Indian Outdoors (www.gio.in) for a day trek to Tungnath-Chandrashila and other hikes around this region.

What You'll Need in the Mountains

- Layered clothing, including a thermal base layer, which will allow you to remove some layers when it's hot and add them when you feel cold
- Sunglasses with holding strings
- A woollen cap
- Comfortable trekking shoes
- A light day knapsack
- Gloves
- Sunscreen lotion
- Some nuts and dry food
- Plenty of water

Acknowledgements

Isn't it fun when you can find a great buddy to go with you on all your adventures? I've been really lucky to find that person. It's my husband, Vaibhav! I can't thank him enough for being the most exciting partner in crime. I've lost count of the number of adventures we've been on together and the number of strange, funny and memorable people we've met. It's because of him that I can chat with just about anyone and make loads of friends while travelling. We've covered only a slice of the world so far, but our list of places runs long. I'm sure it will be a lifetime of fun discovering more unique places together.

Lucky for me, my parents and my sister (despite being scared that I travel alone a lot) have been very supportive of my wanderings. (Of course, I always have to let them know what I'm up to.) It's fabulous to know that someone has your back at all times. Thanks to my brother-in-law, Rajiv, who is a treasure trove of ghost stories and offbeat destinations. He makes sure that my bucket list of places gets longer every time we meet.

A huge dollop of gratitude to Nimmy Chacko, the most patient editor I know, for gently prising these stories out of me to make this book. And the wonderful Niyati Dhuldhoya for scrubbing it clean so it reads this way. Many thanks to the book's designer, Sharanya Kunnath, whose imaginative illustrations give a real peek into what these places look like. It's as if she actually went along with me on these trips!

And a very special thanks to all the people who feature in this book or have helped a story come alive in some way or the other. Nalin, Nandini, Sukanya and Gayatri for their love for the mountains, which they've so graciously shared with me. To Ahalya and Meethil for giving me a quiet corner at Trilogy Library and Bookstore when I was so distracted and needed to write a story quickly (the one on Tiger Falls is for you). To my parents for being the most patient, curious and amazing travel mates in the Andamans. Thanks to Jobin and Scaria for such a comfy stay at Spice Routes Luxury houseboats and helping me catch the Nehru Trophy Snake Boat race in the backwaters in Alleppey. Tightest hugs to Sharon and Govind from Blue City Walks in Jodhpur for digging out the weirdest anecdotes and taking me around, and Jaspreet and Awesh for helping me uncover the secrets of Chhattisgarh.

Also by Supriya Sehgal

A Tigress Called Machhli
and Other True Animal Stories from India

Meet the superstars of India's animal kingdom!

A crocodile who loves eating rice. A mule who won an award for bravery. A photogenic tigress who ruled Ranthambore. Swashbuckling monitor lizards. Rats believed to be the children of a goddess. Cuddly dogs who help nervous travellers. Five thousand punctual parrots... These and many other curious creatures, along with their equally curious human friends, inhabit the pages of this very curious book. Soar, crawl, hop and scamper about with them as they take you on a most unusual journey around the country.

Cheerfully told and charmingly illustrated, these animal stories, collected from cities, jungles, rescue missions and maybe even your own neighbourhood, are funny, fascinating and downright adorable. And the best part? They're all completely true!